DELTA TEACHER DEVELOPMENT SERI

Series editors Mike Burghall and Lindsay Clandfield

Film
in Action

Teaching language using moving images

Kieran Donaghy

Published by
DELTA PUBLISHING
Quince Cottage
Hoe Lane
Peaslake
Surrey GU5 9SW
England

www.deltapublishing.co.uk

© Delta Publishing 2015

ISBN 978-1-909783-07-2

Edited by Mike Burghall
Designed by Christine Cox
Cover photo © iStockphoto.com/liangpv
Film reel illustration: © iStockphoto.com/MarsBars
Printed in China by RR Donnelley

Dedication

I dedicate the book to my wife Noemí,
and our two daughters, Rosa and Aina.

Acknowledgements

I owe a huge debt to Nick Robinson for helping to get this project off the ground, and to Anna Whitcher for her support and encouragement throughout.

I would also very much like to thank Nick Boisseau and Lindsay Clandfield for their belief in me and commitment to the project. In addition, I'm grateful to Christine Cox for her excellent design, and Helen Beesley for her help in promoting the book.

A very special thankyou goes to my editor Mike Burghall, who is everything a writer could wish for in an editor: patient, enthusiastic, encouraging and perceptive. The book would not be half what it is without him.

From the author

My earliest memories of film are going to the Saturday morning matinee shows at the Kingsway Picture House on Kings Heath High Street, Birmingham, UK, with my older brother Loz.

We paid our entrance fee, watched the film, applauded, shouted and screamed with the rest of the boisterous audience in the beautiful neo-classical cinema, and when we particularly liked the film – *Butch Cassidy and the Sundance Kid* and *Bedknobs and Broomsticks* spring to mind – we hid under the seats after our session had finished until the next one started, so we could watch the film again – for free.

I was hooked!

Little did I know that, years later, my passion for film would play a huge role in my professional life as an English language teacher and writer.

Throughout school and university, I regularly went to the cinema – and became a bit of a film buff. When I became a teacher, I quickly saw the benefits of using film in the classroom.

In the 1990s, I remember diligently creating my own materials for films such as *To Kill a Mockingbird*, *Vertigo*, *Rear Window*, *Four Weddings and a Funeral* and *My Fair Lady*. Wherever I taught – whether it was Madrid, Birmingham, Cagliari, Porto, London or Barcelona – my students used to love the films and really seemed to engage with the material.

I continued writing my own film guides and showing films I had a passion for, but I never took my interest in film in language education any further.

Then two things happened, which profoundly changed the way I saw the role of film in language teaching.

Firstly, I discovered Jamie Keddie's pioneering *TEFL Clips* (later to become *Lessonstream*) which was the first online resource to use video clips critically and creatively in language teaching. Jamie opened my eyes to the possibilities of using online video.

Then, one day, I discovered Vimeo and found hundreds of high-quality short films with innovative narrative structures. Now I could really see how to take my passion for using film forward.

There was no looking back!

Since then, I have created my own resource site – *Film English* – which provides lesson plans designed around short films and has won a British Council ELTons Award for Innovation in Teacher Resources. I have written many articles on film, set up an *English through Film* course at my university language school, run numerous workshops, and presented keynote and plenary sessions on film in language teaching at conferences in many countries.

The next logical step was to write a methodology book on how to use film in language education – and set up a website to support it.

I'm delighted to say: here they are – *Film in Action*.

Happy reading and watching!

Kieran

Contents

Contents

'Films have the power to raise your gaze and raise your game and give you a ticket to pleasure and enlightenment forever more ...'

Lindsay Mackie, journalist and film critic

Film in action

Film was considered the great art form of the twentieth century and was undoubtedly one of the most popular. Film, in the twenty-first century, remains one of the most enjoyed and accessible forms of entertainment and artistic expression throughout the world.

Part of its popularity lies in the way it has interacted with other, long-established art forms, including storytelling, music and the visual arts.

However, film is much more than just a popular art form.

Let us consider the following observations:

- *'Film works as a motivator. Film is fun. And film is the rising language of the twenty-first century, whether we want it to be or not. We might as well start embracing it now.'*
  Stephen Apkon [2]
- *'Moving images can educate and inform as well as entertain. In the 21st century, the ability to read critically and evaluate moving images has become an integral part of literacy.'*
  Story of the Movies [3]
- *'Films can enhance the language learning process by designing a series of activities that can develop linguistic, cultural and intercultural skills, as well as developing the practices of New Media Literacies that learners need for the 21st century.'*
  Deborah Chan and Carmen Herrero [4]

In this book, I will be referring to major film and media researchers' findings, and I will try to supply answers to these important questions:

- What is the role of film in society?
- What is the role of film in education?
- What is the relationship between film and literacy in the twenty-first century?
- Why is it becoming increasingly important to help young people analyse films and to educate them in making their own films?
- What are the educational benefits of not just watching film, but also of creating moving images?
- What are the key strategies to use film 'in action' in language teaching, both inside the classroom and outside?

□ □ □

'People do not learn better when tasks are made easier: they learn better when they are encouraged to push back the boundaries of what they already know, and step on to new ground.'

Cary Bazalgette [1]

A key goal of *Film in Action* is to challenge teachers to reflect on the role of film in society, in our educational system and in language learning, and to think more systematically and deliberately about the different ways we might use film critically and creatively – both in the classroom and beyond.

Film in society

'To be a functioning adult in a mediated society, one needs to be able to distinguish between different media forms and know how to ask basic questions about everything we watch, read, or hear.'
Elizabeth Thoman and Tessa Jolls [5]

'We are awash in a world of screens and moving images.'
Stephen Apkon [6]

In today's society, we acquire the majority of our information through moving image media: the cinema, the television, the internet, and the screens that surround us where we work, shop, travel, socialise, and learn. Film is very much at the heart of these moving image media, which are an important and valuable part of our culture.

Technological developments, such as the advent of the internet and the digital revolution, the proliferation of mobile devices which allow us to capture moving images easily, the introduction of cheap and accessible video-editing tools and the emergence of video-sharing sites such as YouTube and Vimeo, have changed forever the way moving images relate to society.

The moving image has extended its reach from the conventional cinema and television screens *'to a myriad of different platforms, yet, whatever the technology, the end product remains the same – stories told, using sound and light that move across a screen'.* [7]

'We have barely begun to explore the place of the moving image in our cultures.'
Andrew Goodwyn [8]

As Stephen Apkon has said: *'What we are now seeing is the gradual ascendance of the moving image as the primary mode of communication around the world: one that transcends languages, cultures and borders. And what makes this new era different from the dawn of television is that the means of production – once in the hands of big-time broadcasting companies with their large budgets – is now available to anyone with a camera, a computer and the will.'* [9]

Developments

So the significance of the moving image is changing profoundly – *'it has developed from being a vehicle for art and entertainment to become a key part of how we communicate, socialise, learn, and do business'.* [10]

'Today everyone's a film-maker.'
Wim Wenders [11]

As Apkon notes, a computer – or even a mobile phone owner – is, potentially at least, in a *producing* role – no longer solely a consumer, but with the capability to edit or create moving images. The fact that children and young people have access to technology which allows them to become media producers in their own right has important consequences for our society and educational system.

It would seem, therefore, to make sense for schools to focus on the moving image and capitalise on learners' knowledge and enthusiasm. However, many teachers believe that a focus on core issues in the curriculum does not allow time for films and television. Furthermore, there is a tendency in society to assume that moving image media are bad for children and could detract from 'real' education.

Dangers

Many people, including some teachers, believe that there exists a direct relationship between a perceived fall in literacy standards and a rise in children's consumption of the moving image, in particular film, television and online video.

In fact, firstly, as Andrew Goodwyn states [12], *'there is currently no actual evidence that the world is becoming a less literate or less sophisticated place'.* And secondly, a negative co-relational effect between media consumption and literacy is not substantiated by empirical study.

"A new generation of media-makers and viewers are emerging which could lead to a sea change in how media is made and consumed.'
Andrew Blau [14]

Indeed, empirical research suggests a more positive relationship between the moving image and print literacy. For example, Margaret Mackey has pointed out [13] the variety and depth of reader engagement with 'moving image texts'. She has shown how they offer children insights into structural aspects of narrative, as it is conveyed through the medium of the moving image.

Definitions

At this point, it would seem to be opportune to clarify two concepts that are recurrent throughout *Film in Action*:

- **Text** has traditionally referred to a book or other written or printed work. However, here, we use the term 'moving image text' to refer to feature films, clips, short films and videos, as well as learner-generated content. They are *texts*, in the same way that books are texts – in the sense that they can be read (analysed and interpreted) and written (created).
- **To read** has been used for centuries to refer to the action of decoding and understanding written or printed texts, and **to write** has conventionally referred to the ability to communicate in writing or print. In this book, we use the term 'read the screen' to mean *to analyse and interpret moving image texts*, and the term 'write the screen' to mean *to make moving image texts*.

Film in education

'*Film and the electronic media have drastically changed the way we perceive the world – and ourselves – during the past century, yet we all too naturally accept the vast amounts of information they convey to us in massive doses without questioning how they tell us what they tell.*'
James Monaco [16]

On the whole, our educational systems have been slow to respond to the new visual technologies and the ascendance of the moving image in our society.

In the words of Andrew Goodwyn: '*Given the prominence of the moving image in twentieth century culture, and the current evidence that it seems to be even more dominant in the twenty-first, it may seem more peculiar that its study is not at the heart of a postmodern education.*' [17]

To better understand the slow reaction of our educational systems to the new visual technology and the dominance of the moving image, we need to explore the concept of literacy and its impact on our educational systems.

Literacy

The concept of literacy is currently undergoing a radical change. Literacy has been traditionally linked to an alphabet or a language code – that is, through reading and writing – and linked with print media. There has been a strong dependence on linguistic theories to define literacy. Consequently, education has been dominated for centuries by written language and by print in particular.

For a long period, the book was the dominant medium of communication. However, with the challenge of a technologically evolving landscape and the ascendance of the image, particularly the moving image, the screen has taken that place.

According to Gunther Kress, a prominent member of the New London Group, a group of scholars who argue that literacy pedagogy should be linked to the rapidly-changing social, cultural and technological environment: '*The former constellation of medium of book and mode of writing is giving way, and in many domains has already given way, to the new constellation of medium of screen and mode of image.*' [19] It is necessary to point out here that this change does not spell the death of the written word. As Kress states: '*Writing is too useful and valuable a mode of representation and communication – never mind the enormous weight of cultural investment in this technology.*' [20]

Communication through visual media will never completely displace reading and writing, as Andrew Goodwyn points out: '*it might be far more productive to consider cultural assimilations rather than replacements.*' [21] We need to expand our competences, rather than shed the old skills to make way for the new ones.

However, the fact that the book has now been superseded by the screen in the role of dominant medium of communication does mean the definition of literacy as decoding print is now outdated.

In the words of Carey Jewitt: *'As a consequence it is no longer possible to think about learning and literacy solely as 'linguistic' accomplishments: the time for that habitual conjunction of 'language and learning' is over. This has significant implications for communication, creativity, education and the design of social futures for the twenty-first century.'* [22]

Multiliteracies

The term 'multiliteracies' was coined by the New London Group, who called for *'a much broader view of literacy than portrayed by traditional language-based approaches'.* [23]

According to Andrew Goodwyn, the multiliteracy movement argues *'for the notion of intellectual tools, ie ways of interpreting the world that have been developed through formal and informal learning. Language and its associated literacy is one tool, but the visual literacy of images and codes is another and both involve the other'.* [24]

The notion of multiliteracies suggests a repertoire of overlapping literacies, and that the acquisition of any literacy leads to the capacity to develop others.

In *Literacy in the New Media Age* [25] Gunther Kress offers a new theory of literacy where he argues that our previous dependence on linguistic theories to define literacy is now obsolete and deficient, and that we must combine language-based theory with semiotics (the study of signs and symbols and how they are used) and other visual theories, to provide an appropriate meaning to the term 'literacy' in the twenty-first century.

Carey Jewitt concludes: *'there is a need to approach literacy practices as an inter-textual web of contexts and technology, rather than isolated sets of skills and competences. … what is needed is an educational framework that recognises and describes the new forms of text that children meet every day in order to secure the place of multimodal and visual texts within the curriculum.'* [27]

Visual literacy

As literacy, in its broadest sense, now reflects a wider cultural competence, the immensely important role of film in our culture and society should be sufficient justification for ensuring their integration in our educational systems.

According to a report by the British Film Institute [28]:
'We live in a world of moving images. To participate fully in our society and its culture means to be as confident in the use and understanding of moving images as of the printed word. Both are essential aspects of literacy in the twenty-first century. In the same way that we take for granted that society has a responsibility to help children to read and write – to use and enjoy words – we should take it for granted that we help children and young people to use, enjoy and understand moving images; not just to be technically capable but to be culturally literate too.'

The importance of visual literacy in education is widely acknowledged. It is generally agreed that education needs to develop learners' skills and ability to interpret image and to communicate visually, and in schools there is a gradual move away from a reliance on print as the primary medium of dissemination and instruction towards visual media and the screen.

When we look at visual literacy, it is necessary to understand both *media* literacy and *film* literacy:
- **Media literacy** is defined by The Media Literacy Centre as follows:
  'a twenty-first century approach to education. It provides a framework to access, analyze, evaluate, create and participate with messages in a variety of forms – from print to video to the Internet. Media literacy builds an understanding of the role of media in society as well as essential skills of inquiry and self-expression necessary for citizens of a democracy.' [29]
- **Film literacy**, which can be considered a subset of media literacy, is defined as follows:
  'the level of understanding of a film, the ability to be conscious and curious in the choice of films; the competence to critically watch a film and to analyse its content, cinematography and technical aspects; and the ability to manipulate its language and technical resources in creative moving image production.' [30]

'Literacy is the repertoire of knowledge, understanding and skills that enable us to participate in social, cultural and political life.'
British Film Institute [26]

While media education has a wider scope than film education, the aims of both are virtually identical – to foster a wider literacy, which incorporates cultural experience, aesthetic appreciation, critical understanding and, increasingly, creative production.

An increasing number of educational theorists stress the importance of both media and film literacy as fundamental to literacy in the twenty-first century – if young people are to be able to participate fully in our society.

However, media literacy and, more particularly, film literacy are still absent from, or on the margins of, national and international policy agendas. While the 'traditional' arts such as music, art and literature have long been established as core elements of national curricula in many countries, film education has typically been ignored.

This absence or marginalisation of film literacy in our educational systems is commented on by many influential writers and film directors. Let us consider the following observations:

- *'You have to make room for film in curriculum. What you are doing is training the eye and the heart of the learner to look at film in a different way by asking questions and pointing to different ideas, different concepts.'*
  Martin Scorsese [32]
- *'Cine literacy is long overdue in American education. The average American watches seven hours of TV per day. Yet, for the most part, we watch them uncritically, passively, allowing them to wash over us, rarely analysing how they work on us, how they can shape our values.'*
  Louis Giannetti [33]
- *'So long as the schools neglect this art form, the audience will be at the mercy of those who seek to manipulate them and will remain intellectually impoverished in an art form that is closer to them than many others.'*
  John Culkin [34]

There is a lack of understanding by policy makers about the importance of film in young children's lives and, as a consequence, in our educational systems. There is also a lack of a structured, systematic opportunity for learners to watch, analyse, interpret and understand films, and even less opportunity for learners to make their own films as part of their overall preparation for adult life.

Social literacy

If learners are to successfully meet the social, cultural, political and economic demands of their futures, they need to be able to read and write in all forms of communication. George Lucas asks the pertinent question: *'If learners aren't taught this new language of sound and images shouldn't they be considered as illiterate as if they left college without being able to read and write?'* [35]

And Stephen Apkon states that, with the ascendance of the moving image and visual technologies, *'our work lives will be changed forever, and soon it will be as unfathomable not to know how to make a video as it is not to know how to send an email'.* [37]

Education has always been focused on preparing young people for their future roles as citizens and workers. We teach children to read and write, not so that they become the next J. K. Rowling or Ian McEwan, although some of them do become professional authors, but so that they can become fully active and participating citizens in society.

The same applies to film.

We should teach children to 'read the screen' – to analyse and interpret moving image texts – and to 'write the screen' – make their own moving image texts – not so that they become the next Kathryn Bigelow or Quentin Tarantino, although some of them will become professional film-makers, but to prepare them for their future roles as citizens and workers in society.

Educating children and young people to be film literate is about democratic entitlement and civic participation. The skills needed for the modern day workplace are quite different from what they were even twenty years ago, yet our educational systems seem to be caught in a time trap.

In our schools, we urgently need the introduction of structured, systematic opportunities for learners to watch, analyse, interpret and understand films, and opportunities for learners to make their own films as part of their overall preparation for life.

A new literacy

The concept of literacy is also changing because of the advent of remix and participatory culture:

- **Remix** is a collage or a recombination of existing images, video clips or music from popular digital culture, 'mashed up' into something new. In other words, a remix is made when a person joins separate media elements to form a new, different piece of media with a different meaning from the original. For example, a young girl in Mexico sees a clip from a Hollywood film she loves and sets it to music which she think suits it; she mixes the original clip with the song and creates a new piece of media.
  A remix culture is one which encourages these derivative works, which combine or edit existing artistic materials to create new products. Copyright scholar Larry Lessig has argued that remix is literacy in the twenty-first century, and a form of self-expression that should be allowed to flow without restriction across today's digital world. [38]

- **Participatory culture** is a global phenomenon whereby young people all over the world are embracing the expressive and distribution resources of digital technologies and the internet, to create and share their own cultural materials with each other. For example, a young man sees a viral video on YouTube which he hates; he creates his own parody of the video and uploads it to YouTube as a response to the original video.
  Scholar Henry Jenkins explains that *'participatory culture describes a world where everyone participates, where we take media in our own hands, and where we have the capacity often to produce media and share media'.* [40] According to Jenkins, *'young people have a richer intellectual and creative life outside of school than inside'.* [41]
  In participatory culture, the focus of literacy shifts from one of individual expression to community involvement. A growing body of research suggests the potential benefits of participatory culture, including the development of skills valued in the twenty-first century workplace.

Scholarship is also beginning to show how elements of remix and participatory culture are part of the process by which children develop literacy in the new century. Jenkins concludes: *'Access to this participatory culture functions as a new form of the hidden curriculum, shaping which youth will succeed and which will be left behind as they enter school and the workplace.'* [42]

Therefore, it is important that young people learn how to create their own media, especially moving image texts, to be able to take part in this remix and participatory culture which will become an increasingly important part of literacy.

Our schools need to help learners to acquire the skills they need to become full participants in our society.

Education in film

'Film education can encompass both watching and making films, and the best kind of film education engages learners in active learning. It goes beyond just passively consuming or watching films.'
Kenneth Brannagh [43]

Film literacy, as we have suggested, involves being able to analyse and interpret moving image texts (*reading the screen*) and being able to edit and make moving image texts (*writing the screen*). Meaning is communicated through moving images more readily than print because of its immediacy, making film literacy an incredibly powerful teaching tool.

'More and more literacy experts are recognizing that enacting, reciting, and appropriating elements from pre-existing stories is a valuable and organic part of the process by which children develop cultural literacy.'
Henry Jenkins [39]

Teaching and learning

Educational programmes that make use of visual and digital media, and show learners how to make their own visual texts, will better prepare learners for their futures in a rapidly-changing world because, when we are educated in the art of film-making, we see that it develops many of the life skills – such as communication, creativity, collaboration, innovation, conflict management and decision making – that are increasingly valued in the modern-day workplace.

In the words of Stephen Apkon [44]:
'Over the past decade, visual storytelling has become one of the new important communication tools for those who want to succeed in business. This is no surprise. The core skill we need almost regardless of profession is communication. It is how we learn, how we share information, and how we build professional relationships and communities. As screens multiply around us and permeate our environments, it is reflected in how we do business.'

In this swiftly-changing world, skills in creativity will be paramount, and visual technologies give young people unique opportunities to be creative in a variety of media. People who can read a variety of texts critically, and who can produce texts in a range of media, will be best equipped to succeed as citizens and workers in our increasingly complex technological world.

And given that the new visual technologies allow people not just to consume media, but to become media producers in their own right, giving learners the opportunity to produce their own media texts is an essential part of this process, on whatever scale is possible.

Carey Jewitt states:
'The creation of user-generated content is a central aspect of technologised production practices for pedagogy. Different forms of production are required that allow learners to generate and produce their own responses. Learner production is an important aspect of learner work in the classroom and research has repeatedly shown the value of production as a kind of externalisation in supporting learning. The work of production forces learners to express their thinking, thereby making the gaps in their knowledge explicit, and clarifying what they need to learn.' [46]

Practical film work is an excellent way for learners to develop an understanding of how moving image conventions work.

It is clear that producing moving image texts is intrinsically motivating and meaningful to learners in our multimedia and multimodal world – in which remix and participatory culture is playing an increasingly important role, as we have seen.

Teaching and learners

There is an urgent need for schools to develop programmes that teach learners not only how to read the screen, but also how to write the screen. As the actor and film director Kenneth Brannagh states: *'Critically, culturally and creatively, film is a key literacy skill for young people. Every young person should have the opportunity to watch films, to learn from them and to make them.'* [48]

For any film education programme to work successfully, it needs clear operating principles, such as the 'three Cs' approach adopted in the UK in *The Charter for Media Literacy* [49] which was drawn up in 2005 by the UK Film Council and its partners on the Media Literacy Task Force: the BBC, Channel 4 and Skillset.

It suggested three ways in which a fully active and participating citizen would to be able to engage with media. The 'three Cs' of *The Charter for Media Literacy* are:

- **Cultural access**
  Learners should have the opportunity to choose from a broad range of films and so get a better understanding of their culture and other people's culture, way of life and history.
- **Critical understanding**
  Learners should become confident enough to look behind the surface of the screen, to understand a film's intentions, techniques and qualities.

■ **Creative activity**

Learners should have the opportunity to make film and moving image texts, to have some understanding of the technical and creative process that allows the effective expression of a story, a mood or an idea.

Part of the reason for the absence or marginalisation of film education training in our schools *'springs from the sense that the school day is already bursting at its seams, that we cannot cram in any new tasks without the educational system breaking down altogether'*. [51]

For that reason, film literacy should not be treated as an optional extra or an add-on subject. Every school subject, including foreign languages, needs to take responsibility for helping learners to master the skills and knowledge they need, to be fully active and participating citizens in our media-saturated society.

We are, therefore, not only talking about 'film in education' but *also* about 'education in film' – as parts of a new educative philosophy.

Brief history of using film in education

'I believe that the motion picture is destined to revolutionise our educational system and that in a few years it will supplant largely, if not entirely, the use of textbooks.'
Thomas Edison [53]

In 1922, Edison, the inventor of one of the first motion picture cameras, made this prediction. Edison's prognostication was, to say the least, overly optimistic.

Although film has been used in education since the 1920s, and while there has been a gradual shift toward visual media and the screen in more recent history, there is still a dependence on print as the primary medium of dissemination and instruction in our educational systems.

Nor has film always been used optimally in schools. Until as recently as the 1970s, *'although moving image texts were having an enormous impact on society, teachers were in general very conservative in their approach'*. [54]

On the margins

In literature education, which is probably the discipline which has the longest tradition of use of moving image texts, film is often used as a guilty pleasure, a treat or a reward after reading a book.

So the learners watch the film adaptation after reading the book, and then the film is compared, usually unfavourably, to the 'original' text, the book. A typical scenario is that learners read a classic book over a reasonable period of time, and then watch the film adaptation in class, often in a single sitting.

The film is not normally treated as a text for study in its own right, and is often perceived as inferior to the written text.

As Andrew Goodwyn points out, there are two key problems with this approach:
'First, it perpetuates the myth that the written text is not only the original, but is also the only valuable version of that narrative, therefore the 'visualization' is a simple and easy version. Second, this approach transmits to pupils the idea that reading literature is always hard work and dull while watching is easy and enjoyable.' [55]

Another subject area which has a long tradition of using film is History. Here, film has probably been used more successfully than in literature education as many history teachers have recognised that the use of films, documentaries and newsreel footage helps learners to 'see' history in a way unlike any other source, making events and people 'real'.

In general, then, until quite recently, film was on the margins of curricula and educational agendas.

In the mainstream

However, as delivery technologies have advanced from film reels to the versatility of videos, DVDs and laserdiscs, this has meant that teachers, essentially for the first time, could easily bring film into the classroom. Additionally, with the advent of digital video, streaming and the emergence of video sharing sites such as YouTube and Vimeo, whereby teachers and learners can watch film and video anytime and anywhere they have internet access, the use of film in the classroom has risen steadily over the last 30 years.

Video streaming signifies that teachers can now show a film without having to locate the film in a library or buy it, reserve the equipment needed to play it on or fight for the only copy of it in the staffroom. Teachers can search for the content they need on any computer with an internet connection, find the content they need from a myriad of resources, and play it at their convenience.

Nowadays, film has gradually been integrated across the curriculum and many teachers use a wide range of methods for using films in the classroom in literature, language learning, history, geography, science and social studies. Most teachers use documentaries or feature films – as 'enrichment' – to enhance their coverage of subject areas.

As visual technologies continue to grow both more sophisticated and more user-friendly, teachers continue to become ever more adept at integrating film into their teaching repertoire. A variety of research studies show that using film in the classroom is a highly-valued means of teaching more effectively and creatively.

For example, in the United States over a period of 20 years, the Corporation for Public Broadcasting conducted surveys of classroom uses of moving images that revealed increased use of, and satisfaction with, moving images in the classroom. In the most recent survey – at the time of writing – 92% of teachers said that using moving images helped them teach more effectively, and 88% more creatively. [58]

Today, Thomas Edison's vision of moving images supplanting textbooks in our schools may not seem so far-fetched. However, despite the fact that many teachers are using film in their classes, learners are not usually encouraged to think critically about the film itself and look beyond the surface of the screen to consider the film's intentions and techniques.

There is still a long way to go, until our classrooms fully reflect the media-rich world our learners live in – and the benefits of preparing learners adequately for this new world.

'Since filmstrips were first studied during World War II as a training tool for soldiers, educators have recognized the power of audio-visual materials to capture the attention of learners, increase their motivation and enhance their learning experience.'
Emily Cruse [57]

'Teachers make use of video and films in the classroom because these materials can help explore cultural context, are easy to integrate into the curriculum, and allow flexibility of materials and teaching techniques.'
Renee Hobbs [59]

Benefits of using film in education

'The study of the moving image will be different from its mere presence in the classroom as adornment or entertainment.'
Andrew Goodwyn [60]

If we want to integrate film fully into the curriculum, it is essential that its use is pedagogical – not decorative. When schools successfully integrate film into the curriculum, it helps them to achieve their educational objectives.

Many teachers recognise that film adds an extra dimension to the curriculum. As film communicates in a range of ways – through speech, the written word, music, sound and physical actions – it gives teachers the ability to develop the achievement of learners of all abilities. Many teachers who use film in education see it as a source of enthusiasm to learners, which leads to improved academic performance and social interaction, as a tool to enhance reading and writing skills, and as a way to boost learners' creativity.

Inspiration

A much cited reason for using film in education is its inspirational quality. Teachers have known for decades that films are popular with young people, who are enthused by the stories they tell. The fact that film can inspire learners is partly because one of the greatest strengths of film *'is the ability to communicate with viewers on an emotional, as well as a cognitive, level'.* [61]

Teachers are increasingly aware that the ability of film to inspire makes it a valuable tool to re-engage learners with the curriculum and increase their overall motivation for learning. More and more teachers are using films to motivate and engage learners in the classroom, as well as to contextualise various areas of the curriculum. In a survey of teachers in 'Film: 21st Century Literacy' in 2010, 100% agreed (or strongly agreed) that film is a means of getting children enthusiastic about their subject. [62]

We know that watching film can help impact positively on academic achievement and help learners to enjoy school more. Using film can also embolden and encourage isolated or disaffected pupils to participate more in class and increase their confidence. The ability of film to galvanise learners can also contribute to increased positive social interaction.

Beeban Kidron, the film director and co-founder of the charity Film Club, which gives over 200,000 children a week in over 7,000 schools throughout the UK the opportunity to watch, discuss and review films, comments on how film inspires learners in different ways [64]:
'We guessed that film, whose stories are a meeting place of drama, music, literature and human experience, would engage and inspire the young people participating in Film Club. What we could not have foreseen was the measurable improvements in behavior, confidence and academic achievement. Once-reluctant learners now race to school, talk to their teachers, fight, not on the playground, but to choose next week's film – young people who have found self-definition, ambition and an appetite for education and social engagement from the stories they have witnessed.'

While film use is an effective educational tool for all learners, its positive effect on special populations of learners is gaining greater attention. There is an increasing body of empirical research that shows that moving image texts are very effective at reaching and empowering children with learning disabilities or economic disadvantages. In one study, a teacher commented:
'All of our children have learning disabilities and filmmaking gives them a way of being creative where they are not judged for their academic skills.' [66]

The ability of film to inspire increases even more when learners are actively involved in making their own moving image texts. Learners are usually highly enthusiastic, and prepared to put in a huge amount of time and effort when working on a movie image project because it is their own and it has a tangible result. Even learners who are normally disaffected and disengaged are happy to work on moving image projects in their own time, and often achieve excellent results.

Integration

Many educational theorists emphasise the significance of linking *learner* knowledge with *school* knowledge. Successful teachers know it makes sense to build on what children already know and can do.

Moving image texts are central to young learners' development of knowledge. Children come to school with a high level of existing knowledge about moving image media. They have learned another language, in addition to their spoken mother tongue: they have learned the codes and conventions through which moving images tell stories, as they have watched thousands of hours of film, television and video.

These young learners with a high level of existing knowledge, which they have gained from and about moving image texts, can often talk about these texts very knowledgeably:

- **Reading skills** In order to help these young learners read printed texts, it is necessary to work with the very texts they are already reading. Their ability to read moving image texts enhances their ability to read all kinds of texts, both in school and outside.
  As David Buckingham states, teachers should therefore encourage learners *'to build upon the knowledge to develop new insights'.* [68]

Print and moving image texts share many common textual strategies. Both print and moving image texts:

- tell stories;
- differentiate between fact and fiction;
- present characters;
- convey a sense of place and context;
- include generic features that help us to recognise certain types of stories.

Research also shows there are many connections between the processes involved in reading print texts and moving image texts. For example, Muriel Robinson [70] has shown that children who are able to draw on these connections and parallels between moving image texts and print texts are more likely to become confident and critical readers across different media, including print.

The concept of narrative is fundamental in linking print and moving image media. By exploring how a moving image text 'tells a story', children use the concrete examples of the visual to develop their comprehension of the more abstract nature of written texts. Children's understanding of narrative structure, and their ability to develop understanding of characterisation and plot, are similar for both print and moving image texts. Thus, print literacy and moving image literacy are not mutually exclusive, but can be developed alongside each other to mutual benefit to enhance learners' understanding of all texts.

Teachers are increasingly recognising that moving image education has a vital role to play in developing the 'higher order' skills – such as analytical thinking, critical thinking, creative thinking and self-reflection – that learners need, to read and understand print and other types of text.

- **Writing skills** Furthermore, teachers are becoming aware that using moving image texts can help learners improve their writing skills. Studying film texts can help learners in their attainment in writing in general, and in their vocabulary and text structure in particular. Films can also inspire learners to write, as they foster emotion which can enhance learning. A film can induce virtually any human emotion, from joy to sorrow, from delight to revulsion, from pity to contempt.

When learners watch a film, they may become emotionally involved and, as a result, are motivated to write about their emotional experience. Through this capacity of film to foster emotion, enthusiasm towards writing can be greatly improved.

Film can be used to increase literacy skills when it is used as literature is often used: as a basis for anchoring writing and critical-thinking activities. As specialist in teaching film as literature Michael Vetrie states: *'learners who gain experience in listening, speaking and writing through interaction with film begin to improve radically their reading and writing ability.'* [72]

Importance

Creativity is becoming an increasingly valued skill in the modern-day workplace, and young people who can create texts in a variety of media will be in demand and much more likely to succeed. Film-making is a highly creative process. As Nikos Theodosakis states: *'When students create a film, it is an opportunity for them to develop a vision of what they want to explore and to see how the vision changes or remains the same as they set out and make it happen. It is practice in turning the intangible into the tangible.'* [73]

Communication technologies now provide learners with many more genuine opportunities for authentic expressions and creativity, using moving images in which they become media producers in their own right. As Carey Jewitt points out: *'digital technologies, and visual communication more generally, offer young people new forms of power and agency within the communicational landscape.'* [75]

Digital technologies have fundamentally changed moving image media production and dissemination. The digitisation of moving image media, greater computer capability and broadband internet connection mean that learners can now work collaboratively with moving images.

These digital tools provide new opportunities for learners to create their own moving image texts. Broadcasting and production of moving image media, which is increasingly important with the ascendance of the moving image and remix and participatory culture, is made possible for young people.

In a study as far back as 2005, over 50% of American teenagers said they had created their own media content, and one third of them had shared media they had created on the internet. [76]

Giving learners the opportunity to create their own moving image texts in the classroom is important, as it supports their learning by forcing them to express their thinking and clarify what they need to learn.

This capacity of new technologies to provide young people with creative ways to engage with cultural resources needs to be exploited fully in our schools, by ensuring that learners have the opportunity to *make* moving image texts not just *watch* them.

There has to be a shift in schools towards an emphasis on creative production which takes advantage of the emergence of these new digital tools and the increased access to affordable filming and editing equipment.

> '*When television, video and other media are used with dynamic and vigorous interaction and engagement between learners and teacher, significant learning experiences can result.*'
>
> Renee Hobbs [77]

Benefits of using film in language education

'*The use of film in the classroom or as an outside school activity can uphold the motivation of the learners, because of its playful component.*'
Deborah Chan and Carmen Herrero [78]

One of the main benefits of using film in language teaching is that it is highly motivating and relates to the learners' lives. Learners engage with moving images constantly outside the classroom, are knowledgeable about them, and enjoy watching them.

Motivation

'Motivation' has been identified as one of the most important factors in determining successful second language acquisition.

As watching films and TV series is an integral part of our learners' lives – indeed, one of the main motivations for many learners is to have access to English language films and television series – it makes sense to bring them into the language classroom.

> '*With visual storytelling, we are able to foster a more creative learning environment in our classrooms. Weaker students feel like they have the support from the visuals to express their ideas, and stronger students get the challenge they need to engage with the material at a higher level.*'
>
> Anna Whitcher [79]

Film, as a motivator, also makes the language learning process more entertaining and enjoyable. Films are designed to appeal directly to people's emotions. As Andrew Goodwyn argues [80], '*the focus in the classroom needs to be on educating about film and on engaging the learners' motivation and interest to help them understand and enjoy film even more than they do already*'.

The motivational qualities of film in language learning can be even more enhanced if the learners are encouraged to create their own films. In our multimedia and multimodal world, producing moving image texts is intrinsically motivating to learners. As Ben Goldstein and Paul Driver ask: '*How much more motivational if the learners produce the videos themselves?*' [81]

For many young people, one of their motivations for learning English may well be to create remix videos and other media in English in order to become part of the global participatory culture, which uses English as its lingua franca.

> '*Foreign language teaching must be concerned with reality: with the reality of communication as it takes place outside the classroom and with the reality of learners.*'
>
> William Littlewood [82]

Authentic language

Another vital benefit of using film is that it provides a source of authentic and varied language. Films are authentic material, and provide learners with genuine input which helps them see the foreign language used in 'real' situations outside the classroom.

Krashen points out [83] that a natural input helps learners 'acquire', without necessarily noticing that they are hearing or reading a foreign language. Film can be a useful way to help learners acquire a language rather than learn it consciously.

Film also provides learners with authentically interactive language, the language of real-life conversation. 'Interaction' is recognised in the Common European Framework of Reference for Languages [84] as one of the major areas of language competence, along with Production, Reception and Mediation.

However, interactive language is not normally covered thoroughly in coursebooks, which usually focus on more formal language. As a result, learners are often unable to produce natural spoken English, and have a limited repertoire of functional language and colloquial expressions.

Film exposes learners to these natural expressions and the natural flow of speech. If they are not living in an English-speaking environment, perhaps only film and television can provide them with this real-life language input. As Jane Sherman states [86], learners *need such exposure because to learn to speak to people they must see and hear people speaking to each other'.*

'The combination of sound, vision and language engages and stimulates our senses and cognitive faculties simultaneously, creating a total impact that dwarfs other mediums.'
Alan Maley [85]

Visuality

The visuality of film makes it an invaluable language teaching tool. This visuality means that learners often understand much more because language is interpreted in a full visual context, which helps them by supporting the verbal message and provides a focus of attention while they listen.

Because of the wealth of visual information and stimuli it provides, film contributes to the development of learning strategies such as predicting or guessing from the context, inferring ideas, and a chance to activate background schemata.

Film assists the learners' comprehension by enabling them to *listen* to language exchanges and *see* such visual supports as facial expressions and gestures simultaneously – supporting the message and providing a focus. Weaker learners may also understand more, as they are offered another channel of comprehension.

People learn abstract and new concepts better when presented in both verbal and visual form. Film can make it easier to teach such concepts in the language classroom because of this visuality.

Film is also a good way of teaching vocabulary related to a certain theme by contextualising the vocabulary.

'The ability to capture diverse images, text and sounds and make educated decisions regarding the best way to combine them into a coherent and meaningful product makes digital filmmaking an appropriate tool for creative language learning.'
Seemita Mohanty [87]

Intercultural communication

As films are cultural documents, they are excellent at communicating cultural values, customs, attitudes, behaviour and religious beliefs, and increasing language learners' intercultural understanding.

In the words of Alan Maley: *'Film also offers an enlargement of our knowledge of the world and the cultures it contains. It is in the broadest sense 'educational'.'* [88]

Film has a unique capacity for the development of cultural understanding.

By watching films made and set in their *own* country, learners can better understand their own culture. Watching films made and set in *other* cultures can help them to develop an awareness of sameness and difference which is essential to cultural understanding.

Film has an incredible capacity to bring a wide range of diverse cultural ideas into play in the classroom. Teachers can help to give learners a broader understanding of other cultures by introducing a broad range of film.

'Intercultural communicative competence' refers to the ability to understand cultures, including one's own, and use this understanding to communicate successfully with people from other cultures.

It is increasingly recognised that learning a foreign language involves not only fostering linguistic competence but also intercultural communicative competence, in order to be able to deal effectively and appropriately with cultural diversity.

One of the primary aims of second language acquisition is to facilitate learners to communicate with people from different linguistic and cultural backgrounds.

The importance of intercultural communicative competence in our globalised world is reflected in the Common European Framework of Reference for Languages, which argues that teachers should develop not just their learners' communicative *language* competences, but also their *intercultural* competence. [89]

Using films from the target language culture in the language classroom is a very effective way to help language learners understand different cultures. As Deborah Chan and Carmen Herrero state: *'Films are perfect vehicles for introducing learners to different types of popular culture and engaging them with critical questions about the relationship between information and power, through the critical analysis of sociopolitical issues and intercultural relationships.'* [90]

Variety and flexibility

Film can bring variety and flexibility to the language classroom by extending the range of resources and teaching techniques, helping learners to develop all four communicative skills. This, in turn, provides a framework for classroom communication and discussion, and can ultimately involve the learners in creative film-making projects.

The different roles of film in the language learning classroom can supply the teacher with a variety of techniques. Ben Goldstein and Paul Driver [92] identify four main roles of moving images in language teaching:

- Firstly, there can be a *language focus* – when new or recently introduced words are encountered in context in a film sequence.
- Secondly, film can be used for *skills practice* – a whole film or a sequence is used to practise listening and (to a lesser extent) reading, and as a model for speaking and (to a lesser extent) writing.
- A third role is as a *stimulus* – where film acts as a springboard for follow-up tasks such as discussions, debates on social issues, roleplays, reconstructing a dialogue or summarising.
- The fourth role is as a *resource* – in which the film provides the learners with the content for subsequent tasks which will increasingly involve them in making their own films.

It is possible to bring further variety to the language learning classroom by screening different types of film – feature-length films, short sequences of films, short films, adverts and a whole array of digital video content, as we shall be discussing.

'Using films through specific task activities provides an ideal vehicle for active learning, as well as encouraging interaction and participation.'

Deborah Chan and Carmen Herrero [91]

'Our task now is to keep encouraging our students to become effective communicators and active participants in their language learning. This is going to involve adopting new approaches to language, often integrating what students are already engaging with and learning outside of the classroom.'

Anna Whitcher [93]

'We must teach communication comprehensively in all its forms. We live and work in a visually sophisticated world, so we must be sophisticated in using all the forms of communication, not just the written word.'

George Lucas [94]

Using film in the classroom

Given the many benefits of using film in the language learning classroom, it is not surprising that many teachers are keen to use film with their learners, and an increasing number of them are successfully integrating film into the language leaning syllabus and using film in pedagogically sound ways to engage their learners.

As with all educational technologies, the value of film relies on how it is implemented in the classroom. Effective language learning is greatly enhanced and extended when the film is integrated into the rest of the lesson.

Effectively integrating film into the classroom involves the following:
- Careful selection of topic and content.
- Clear pedagogical goals.
- Thoughtful preparation.
- Staged activities for before, during and after viewing.

This of course is, in essence, similar to other areas of serious pedagogical implementation. And if we wish to integrate film fully into the language classroom, using film is no different.

Content

When choosing a film, teachers should consider if the *theme* of the film fits into the syllabus, age appropriateness, and whether it will be of interest to their learners. Taboo themes in specific cultures are also important to consider when selecting a film.

Selecting effective film is an essential component of integrating this medium into the language classroom. When selecting a film, it is extremely important to consider the level of the *language*:
- At any level, teachers should not underestimate how frustrating it can be for learners to sit through a film, particularly a feature-length film, and understand very little of the dialogue.
- At lower levels, it may sometimes be a good idea to choose short films which are silent or have very little dialogue, so that comprehension does not become a problem.

When evaluating the level of the language of a film, the following factors are worth considering:
Comprehension may be *hindered* by:
- a lot of dialogue and relatively little action – for example, many Woody Allen films;

- more than one character speaking at the same time;
- very loud soundtracks, which make the dialogue difficult to understand;
- dialects and strong regional accents;
- complex storylines. For example, the film *Memento* by Christopher Nolan is very difficult for language learners as it is presented as two different sequences of scenes: a series of scenes in black and white is shown chronologically, and a series of scenes in colour is shown in reverse chronological order.

Comprehension may be *helped* by:
- dialogues with a high degree of visual support, and a close connection between speech and action – for example, a character says *'I need a drink'* and then drinks a beer;
- clear conventional storylines. Romances, romantic comedies and action films often have relatively simple plots and subplots;
- clearly enunciated speech;
- only one character speaking at a time;
- titles, subtitles, graphics and animations.

Another factor to consider when selecting a film is *length*.

Feature-length films often last two hours or more, and watching such a long film in a foreign language may lead to learners experiencing cognitive overload.

Using short films and film clips may make a more optimal use of class time:
- The majority of films and videos on film-sharing sites such as YouTube and Vimeo are between two and five minutes long.
- This dovetails exactly with expert recommendations for video usage, which suggests that, with limited class times, short film clips of two to five minutes will be more useful than longer sequences.

As film is a visual medium, optimal use capitalises on the strengths of its *visual* content.

It is therefore important to select content which is aesthetically pleasing and appeals to the emotions of the learners.

Goals

Having selected a film which is appropriate for age and language level, and which will appeal to their learners, the teacher has to decide upon the pedagogical goals they want to achieve through using the film:
- The clear purposes for viewing a film need to be established.
- The value of a film is closely correlated to how closely the content and educational objectives fit into the overall structure of the class.

Pedagogical goals may be, for instance:
- To use film to introduce or raise awareness of a topic at the beginning of a class.
- To give the learners a chance to see a language point in a 'real life' conversation in a scene.
- To use a short film as a prompt for written or oral communication.

Obviously, in many cases a teacher will have more than one pedagogical goal – these goals don't have to be exclusively raising awareness, language-based or communication-based. For example, the teacher may want to do all the following:
- Help the learners find out more about a theme.
- Give them a chance to see and hear vocabulary they have recently studied.
- Use this vocabulary in a communicative activity designed around the theme of the film.

Preparation

After selecting the film and clearly defining the instructional purposes, the teacher has to decide on the activities and sequence of activities which will accompany the film and ensure that they promote 'active' viewing.

In the language classroom, teachers have traditionally sequenced the use of film in terms of pre-viewing, while-viewing and post-viewing tasks:
- This appears to be a practical, consistent and well-established educational practice.
- This does not therefore need to be altered, as it has worked effectively for many years.

What the teacher can change, however, is the relative emphasis on each of the three stages and the kinds of activities used with the film:
- They can extend a stage in order to achieve their pedagogical goals.
- They can choose activities which will depend on the content of the film and the pedagogical goals of the lesson.

For the sequencing to work well, it is necessary for the teacher to carefully link the stages of a pre-viewing/viewing/post-viewing sequence to one another, and perhaps to previous and subsequent sequences.

Pre-viewing

It is important that the pre-viewing activities prepare the learners for the actual viewing by helping them to follow the film and understand the storyline and characters:
- If the pedagogical goal of the viewing is *language-based*, pre-viewing tasks could include pre-teaching vocabulary or expressions which appear in the dialogue of the film.
- If the instructional purpose of viewing is mainly *communicative*, activities could include pre-viewing discussion tasks which generate prediction, speculation and a chance to activate background schemata about the topic, content or narrative of the film to be viewed.

Viewing

Viewing activities should help the learners to stay *focused* on the film, but not *overload* them.

As it is difficult to watch a film and write at the same time, it is important to set and establish the purpose of the task before viewing, but to tell the learners they can complete the tasks after viewing.

There is a wide range of viewing tasks – which one the teacher selects will depend on the instructional purpose of the lesson. When the teacher chooses a short film or film clip, the film can be viewed several times and a different focus or activity can be used for each viewing:
- If the pedagogical goal is *comprehension*, it is typical to set multiple-choice or true/false comprehension questions, or to give the learners the dialogue with some functional words and expressions taken out, for them to complete.
- If the instructional purpose is *language-based*, a typical activity for this stage is for the learners to complete fill-in-the-blank viewing sheets with the target language – for example, grammatical structure, vocabulary and expressions.

While these activities are perfectly valid, the tasks should preferably not *all* just be language-based or comprehension-based. It is a good idea to also try to include tasks which focus on and exploit other facets of the film – such as the visual, cinematography, sound, culture, genre and narrative:
- If the pedagogical goal is focused on *cinematography*, we may, on this occasion, want to use viewing and taking notes as part of an 'active viewing' strategy.
- If the pedagogical goal is developing *visual skills*, we may show the film with no sound and ask the learners to focus exclusively on what they see and try to understand the story the film tells.
- If the pedagogical goal is to raise the learners' *intercultural awareness*, we may ask them to notice any aspects of the target language culture illustrated in the film which are different from *their* culture.

Post-viewing

Post-viewing activities often involve the learners extracting the main ideas or concepts of the film, or guiding the learners' attention to meaning and production tasks:
- If there is a clear *language* goal, we may want the learners to use, in speaking or writing, the target items they encountered in the film, or to match target expressions with the characters who said them in the film.
- If the instructional purpose of the film viewing is *communicative*, it is important to select follow-up activities which encourage the learners to reflect on and explore the concepts or ideas contained in the film. We should try to get a personal response from the learners which may help to consolidate learning. Among the many possibilities for post-viewing are:

- research projects on ideas/themes brought up in the film;
- small-group discussions on the ideas or issues raised in the film;
- learners writing about how the film makes them feel;
- learners creating their own moving image texts in response to the film.

- If the pedagogical goal has a *cinematic* focus, an excellent post-watching activity is for the learners to discuss open-ended critical questions that involve them in analysing the director's purpose, point of view and methods of developing ideas through language, image and sound.

Using feature-length films

Feature-length films have been used in language teaching for many years, and have generally been used in two ways.

Viewing in one sitting

The first approach is to show the whole film in one sitting:

- When this approach is used, the pre-viewing tasks may include extensive language work on words and expressions contained in the film's dialogue, or discussion of themes the film deals with.
- However, learners are often not asked to perform any tasks – beyond trying to comprehend the film and enjoy it.

Sometimes this approach is taken after the learners have read a novel, and they watch the film to compare the printed text with the moving image text:

- While the learners view the film, they may be asked to consider some questions about the film which they will discuss after watching.
- After watching, the learners may compare the book they have read to the film they have just seen, or discuss the theme of the film, the characters or the narrative.
- Again, they are often not asked to perform any tasks – beyond trying to comprehend the film and enjoy it.

The learners may also be asked to give a personal response to a film, by writing a review or a composition on how the film made them feel.

The advantages of this approach are that learners often enjoy watching films in this way:

- The film is treated as a work of art and shown as the director intended – that is, in one sitting.
- It offers learners extensive exposure to authentic language, and they may pick up very useful functional language and colloquial expressions.

A possible disadvantage of this approach is that learners may find it difficult to concentrate for up to two hours, and this may lead to cognitive overload and learners watching the film passively.

Sometimes, also, this method is used with little or no preparation, and often no pre-watching, while-watching or follow-up activities:

- Showing a whole film in this way is sometimes 'justified' as a 'treat' after a hard week of studying grammar, or to calm down young learners when they become agitated.
- Showing a film in this way – without any clearly-defined pedagogical goals – is better used only occasionally, as it fails to integrate film effectively into the curriculum.

An alternative approach is to do the pre-viewing activities in class, still, but the learners view the film at home:

- While watching the film in the comfort of their own home, they can pause the film and re-watch any scenes they do not understand – which may be beneficial.
- After viewing the film, the learners do the post-viewing activities in class, sharing their opinions of the film with the teacher and their classmates.

This last approach may make more optimal use of class time.

Viewing in several sittings

In the second approach, the learners view the whole film in short sequences over a number of sessions. There are two types of tasks teachers typically use to exploit this approach:

- Firstly, the teacher gives the learners detailed viewing sheets, which they have often diligently prepared themselves on language and cultural features of the film, which the learners have to complete.
- This method is also used as a tool to aid listening comprehension. The learners watch the film and are invited to carry out listening comprehension exercises and activities based exclusively on what is said by the characters or the narrator, in very much the same way as they might with an audio text. These exercise types are usually exactly the same as those used in a listening comprehension task. Typically, learners are given:
  - the dialogue with some functional words and expressions taken out, and they have to complete it;
  - a list of statements which relate to the dialogue, and they have to say whether they are true or false;
  - a number of comprehension questions based on the dialogue, which they have to answer;
  - the transcript of the voice-over, with a number of pieces of incorrect information which they have to correct.

There are two main advantages to this approach:

- Firstly, as the film is shown in short sequences, it is cognitively less challenging for the learners than viewing a whole film.
- Secondly, the sequence can be shown several times, which results in the learners possibly understanding more and engaging with the material on a more meaningful level.

Although this approach is very thorough and pedagogically sound, a possible disadvantage is that it may be very time-consuming for the busy teacher if they create their own viewing sheets for each sequence:

- Any teacher who has ever written their own activities for a film knows it is a very laborious process, which involves watching the film repeatedly and transcribing the dialogue or voice-over.
- Most teachers do not have much time for extra class preparation.

When this approach is used as an aid for *listening*, the great advantage is that it can make understanding easier for learners:

- The setting, actions, body language, gestures, expressions, etc, in a film provide an important comprehension tool.
- The visual support means that learners often understand much more, because language is interpreted in a full visual context which helps them by supporting the verbal message.

Although this approach uses this full visual context to aid *comprehension*, a possible disadvantage is that it fails to exploit the *other* rich visual details of moving image texts. It seems a wasted opportunity not to have any tasks which focus on what the learners have seen:

- Film is a primarily visual medium, and optimal educational use capitalises on its visual richness.
- Film becomes much less effective as an educational tool in language learning if the activities the learners are asked to do depend largely on non-visual elements.

Viewing short film clips

For many years, teachers have enjoyed finding and using film clips (excerpts from feature films) which fit in perfectly with the grammatical point, vocabulary or theme they want to present and practise in class.

The emergence of YouTube in 2005, where we can find hundreds of thousands of film clips, has made it easier to find just the clip we are looking for, and allows for greater flexibility.

There are a number of advantages to this approach:

- The main advantage is that, as the clip is short, the learners can watch it several times, study it in greater depth and engage with it more meaningfully.
- Another advantage is that the teacher is using the type of short visual texts the learners are engaging with outside the classroom.
- A third advantage is that it allows teachers greater spontaneity, as they can find and show clips as themes come up in the class.

The main possible disadvantage of using short film clips is that, when the teacher finds and shows a clip during a class, there may be little or no preparation and no clear pedagogical aims.

Using short films

When the very first films were shown to the public in 1894, through Thomas Edison's Kinetoscope, they were very short films depicting celebrities, travelogues, current affairs and scenes from everyday life.

But from the early 1900s, advances in recording and editing technology allowed film-makers to create longer films, which eventually led to the birth of feature-length films:

- Feature films – seen as more artistic and respectable – became the most popular art form of the twentieth century.
- The short film fell out of favour with commercial cinema.

Renaissance of the short film

However, technological changes – the development of digital video; the proliferation of mobile devices which allow us to easily capture moving images; the introduction of inexpensive and user-friendly editing tools which let us edit moving images proficiently; the emergence of video-sharing sites such as YouTube and Vimeo – have made it easier for people to create and share their own moving image texts, and this has led to the renaissance of the short film.

The internet is an increasingly popular alternative for the makers of short films who cannot afford to distribute their films on DVD:

- Film-makers can post their films online with no expenditure at all – and reach thousands, and potentially millions, of viewers.
- Short films are perfect for internet viewers who want short sharp bursts of entertainment they can watch at work, at home or, increasingly, on the move on their mobile devices.

Rise of the short film in teaching

This ascent of the short film can be exploited in the classroom:

- Most language teachers realise that feature films are too long to be viewed and discussed in ordinary classroom sessions, while short films can be more easily integrated into the language classroom as they are generally between five and 10 minutes in length.
- Teachers also know that short clips from long films do not work well if what we want to do is to understand how complete narrative structures work, or how characters develop over the course of a whole story.

In contrast, as short films tell a whole narrative in a short period of time, it is clear that they are the ideal vehicle for focusing on narrative structure and character development in the language classroom:

- Many short films are often open to many levels of interpretation.
- Most short films are not commercial and, being unfamiliar to learners, they have a great capacity to surprise, inspire, stimulate and provoke.

The rise of short films is likely to continue for quite some time:

- Newer, easier and cheaper ways of creating, distributing and watching short films will continue to develop.
- The entertaining, motivational and inspirational qualities of short films to grab learners' attention are well-documented.
- The use of short films to encourage learners, especially younger ones, to pay attention is an effective and valuable teaching tool:
  - To pique the learners' interest.
  - To motivate them when interest is flagging.
  - To cause an impact to promote discussion and debate.

However, it is important that this approach is not overused, and that we have other educational goals and objectives for using film in the classroom, beyond simply getting the learners' attention.

Reasons for using short films in language teaching

Here are five good reasons:

- Short films are particularly useful to exploit in a single lesson, as they offer a complete narrative in a short space of time, which captures and holds learners' attention. Learners love narratives, and short films tell innovative and creative stories:
  - Short *films* are not necessarily governed by the same conventions as feature-length films.
  - Short film-*makers*, because they are normally independent and not tied to big film studios, often have greater scope for innovation and creativity, which leads to more imaginative forms and narrative structures.
  These departures from more familiar forms and narrative structures very often provoke stronger responses from learners than the more traditional narratives of feature-length films.
- Another characteristic of many modern short films which can be exploited in language teaching is that they are silent or have very little dialogue:
  - As many of these short films are often 'artistic', they have limited appeal in the commercial marketplace and are funded from diverse sources, so to make them easier to sell worldwide, they often contain little or no dialogue, which makes comprehension much easier.
  - As a result, they offer intensely 'filmic' experiences, using images and movement, sequence and duration, sound and music to tell their stories.
  We can get the learners to supply the dialogue, by imaging what the characters are thinking or what they would say.

- Most short films focus on a single idea or make a single statement, which makes them excellent prompts for oral communication:
  - Many short films deal with contemporary subjects and issues such as bullying, racism, sexism, consumerism and human rights, which are not normally covered in coursebooks, which tend to have safer, blander themes.
  - These present-day themes are very relevant to the lives of learners, who are perfectly capable of coping with these subjects.
  The short films which deal with these contemporary issues are excellent beginning points for engaging learners in a wide range of conversational activities such as pairwork and groupwork, discussions and debates, and roleplays – stimulating an active engagement with language.

- Short films are the ideal media for introducing and promoting film literacy (the ability to analyse and interpret moving images):
  - When analysing films, there is a tendency to focus on quite difficult and inaccessible feature films and to over-intellectualise concepts – which is very intimidating for both teachers and learners.
  - Short films are brief, accessible and tell stories that learners understand.
  Being far less intimidating, they help both teachers and learners to become confident enough to look behind the surface of the screen, to understand a film's intentions, techniques and qualities.

- Many teachers are very adept at using film to foster spoken communication, but they do not necessarily use it to encourage their learners to *write*. Short films are excellent prompts for writing activities, such as the following:
  - Writing an alternative ending.
  - Writing a prequel or a sequel.
  - Writing from the perspective of one of the characters.
  Learners find this both engaging and motivating.

To summarise, because of their accessibility, brevity, innovation and creativity, short films are the perfect vehicle for using moving images in the language learning classroom – and for promoting both oral *and* written communication.

Using new film genres

The increasing ease of creating short moving image texts has led to *new* genres which can be easily and successfully exploited in language teaching:

- **Branded shorts** are short films which have been created for a brand or company. For example, search for 'Castello Cavalcanti' on YouTube. Branded shorts are a fusion between advertising and entertainment:

- They are generally entirely funded by the brand or company and have very big budgets, which allows them to use famous directors and actors, and very expensive production techniques. As a result, they are often very slick and look stunning.
- They are excellent in the language classroom, as they grab the attention of the learners, have first-rate acting and innovative narratives.

The fact that they are trying, directly or indirectly, to promote or sell something makes them superb prompts for discussion and debate.

- **Social shorts** are short films which deal with social themes such as poverty, homelessness, discrimination, etc:
  - They are sometimes commissioned by non-governmental organisations or charities, to raise awareness of a particular social problem.
  - They lack the huge budgets of branded shorts, but they are usually very gripping, because they deal with the type of issues which relate to learners' lives, and are very dramatic and emotional.

This fosters learner engagement and enthusiasm to communicate. To see an example of a short that can have a strong impact on learners, search for 'Momentos short film' on YouTube.

- **Viral shorts** are short films that become very popular through being shared rapidly and widely on the internet, typically through film-sharing websites like YouTube and Vimeo, social media and email. For example, search for 'I Forgot My Phone' on YouTube. As they are often funny, strange or powerful:
  - Learners respond strongly to them.
  - They enjoy discussing how they made them feel.

Learners also enjoy writing critiques of these viral shorts, analysing questions such as: *Why is the film so popular? Who does the film appeal to? Would they share the film?*

- **Music shorts** are short films which are created to accompany a song. To see an example, search for 'Jake Bugg Two Fingers' on YouTube. Normally, a record company contracts a film director to create a visual narrative which reflects the lyrics of the song. The singer or different members of the group often appear as actors in these shorts:
  - As they have very big budgets, they look very beautiful and tell interesting stories.
  - As learners often like the singers and bands, they are motivated to watch the film.

These films work very well, as the teacher can exploit and highlight the rich *visual* details by playing the film with the sound off, and exploit the *lyrics* by playing the film with the sound on and asking the learners to reconstruct the lyrics.

- **Infographic films** are animated representations of information, data or knowledge. For example, search for '7 Billion: Are You Typical?' on YouTube. As they present a lot of information in a meaningful, easy-to-understand and attention-grabbing way, they are highly effective in the language classroom. A very simple but effective activity is:
  - The learners note down 10 pieces of information or data as they watch.
  - They then write 10 questions for the 10 pieces of information or data they wrote down.
  - When they are ready, the learners ask their questions to a partner.

As learners are more likely to understand quite complex information, infographic films are effective prompts for both written and oral communication. For example, the learners can discuss the most interesting/surprising/predictable information or data in the film, or write about what conclusions they drew from the video, using the evidence they found to support their conclusions.

- **Animated lectures** are film lectures created by pairing leading experts with talented animators:
  - As these intellectually-challenging but enjoyable films deal with interesting topics and make complex ideas much easier to understand, they are very effective teaching tools in the language classroom.
  - Learners understand much more, as comprehension is facilitated through the input of audio, text and attractive animation.

The films foster communication, as they engage and capture the attention of the learners. To see an example, search for 'RSA Animate Changing Education Paradigms' on YouTube.

- **Split-screen shorts** are films with a visible division of the screen into two halves, with different moving images in each half:
  - There is different action on the two halves of the screen.
  - An obvious way that split-screen shorts can be exploited is to talk about similarities and differences.

As learners watch the film, their task can be to identify these similarities and differences between the action they are seeing on the two sides of the screen. To see an example of a split-screen film, search for 'Splitscreen: A Love Story' on YouTube.

- **Response films** are short films created by a director in response to a branded short film which has 'gone viral'. For example, search for 'Dove Real Beauty Parody' on YouTube. These films normally criticise or parody the content and message of the original film, and are often humorous and hard-hitting:
  - The fact that they offer another perspective on a theme means that they are excellent tools for developing critical thinking skills and encouraging learners to be wary of taking viral films at face value.

□ They make us aware that, when we watch a film, we are often being manipulated by the director.

An excellent way to motivate and engage learners in active learning is to get them to create their own short films in response to a viral film.

■ **New silent short films** can be used for different language levels, as learners don't have to worry about understanding dialogue:

□ Dialogue can be very difficult for lower-level learners, so the stories they tell are easy to understand.

□ Teachers just need to grade the activities to make them level-appropriate for their learners.

As the films have no dialogue, they also give learners the opportunities to supply the language by creating their own written or spoken dialogues. For an example of a silent film, search for 'The Adventures of a Cardboard Box' on YouTube.

■ **Mash-ups** are short films which are montages or combinations of two or more already existing films or videos which usually have no discernible relation with each other. These are combined or 'mashed' to create a single film:

□ A well-known example of a mash-up takes the trailer for Stanley Kubrick's classic horror film *The Shining*. It is combined with another trailer to create a new trailer for a feel-good family film. To see this mash-up, search for 'The Shining Trailer Mash-up' on YouTube.

□ Mash-ups can be used in the classroom to help learners understand the conventions of different genres.

Learners enjoy creating their own mash-ups by combining films from very different genres to create their own unique film.

To summarise, which genre and film you decide to use will depend on your pedagogical goals. But one very effective use of *all* genres of short film is to make the learners sit up – and notice.

We have suggested so far, in Part A of *Film in Action*, that different moving image texts such as whole feature films, clips and short films are excellent resources for teachers to use in the language classroom. They can inspire, expose learners to a wide range of authentic language, aid comprehension, improve intercultural understanding, and help learners develop visual literacy.

As the moving image becomes ever more dominant in our society, *film* and *learner-created film* will become a central focus in the language classroom, and this is one of our ambitious goals in this book: to place moving image texts at the centre of the language learning agenda.

The author recommends ...

There are many websites you can go to, to find out more about film – and discover resources, lesson plans and tools. There is a small selection below that I highly recommend, as well as some highly-recommended books for you to read.

But first, here are my three film sites:

Film in Action – *http://filminaction.com/*
The website which supports the book. It provides examples of the classroom activities and learner-generated films in *Film in Action*, a glossary of film language terms, and advice on where to look online for resources and lesson plans.

Film English – *http://film-english.com/*
The author's award-winning resource site, with more than a hundred detailed lesson plans designed around short films. Many examples of the activities in Part B can be found here.

A Visual Manifesto – *http://visualmanifesto.com/*
A website which hosts a short film made by Anna Whitcher and the author to illustrate how we can become active learners and creators in this new world of images; and a written manifesto which aims to promote visual literacy and place images at the centre of the language learning agenda.

General film websites

The Film Site – *http://www.filmsite.org/*
An award-winning website which supplies detailed plot synopses, review commentary and film reference material.

The Internet Movie Database – *http://www.imdb.com/*
The internet bible for many film buffs. This site contains reviews of thousands of movies, plus biographies of actors and directors.

Film resources

Film Club – *http://www.filmclub.org/*
A UK charity which supplies hundreds of pedagogically-sound free film guides.

Film in Language Teaching Association –
http://www.filta.org.uk/
FILTA is an association of language teachers, film educators and researchers which provides a forum for the exchange of information and material related to the use of film in language teaching.

Film Education – *http://www.filmeducation.org/*
A website that produces engaging film guides for a wide range of films for primary and secondary school children.

ESL Notes – *http://www.eslnotes.com/synopses.html*
A superb resource site, created by Raymond Weschler, which provides over 200 detailed film guides.

The Film Space – *http://www.thefilmspace.org/*
An organisation that provides moving image-related, curriculum-linked resources, as well as providing training and advice on the use of moving image media in the classroom.

Short films

Vimeo Staff Picks – *https://vimeo.com/channels/staffpicks*
A great selection of high-quality short films, hand-selected by the staff at Vimeo.

Future Shorts – *www.youtube.com/futureshorts*
A YouTube channel with hundreds of interesting short films.

Short of the Week – *www.shortoftheweek.com*
A website dedicated to finding the finest short films available online.

Learner film sites

English Attack – *www.english-attack.com/*
Learners can improve their English through this community site, which uses clips from films, TV series and online games.

English Central – *http://www.englishcentral.com*
An innovative site which provides learners with videos with subtitles. The learners watch the videos, record themselves repeating what they hear, and then get feedback on their pronunciation.

Learn English Teens Film UK –
http://learnenglishteens.britishcouncil.org/uk-now/film-uk/
A British Council website which gives learners the opportunity to watch amazing films made by young people and do a variety of activities designed around the films.

Lesson plans and projects

Allat C – *http://allatc.wordpress.com/*
An excellent blog by Steve Muir and Tom Ireland, which provides lesson plans mainly designed around short videos for teachers of advanced learners (CEFR levels C1 and C2).

Lessonstream – *http://lessonstream.org/*
Jamie Keddie's pioneering website has a wealth of lesson plans designed around short videos.

Viral ELT – *http://viralelt.wordpress.com/*
A blog by Ian James, dedicated to exploiting viral videos in language teaching.

Urban Chronicles –
http://digitaldebris.info/urban-chronicles/
Paul Driver's innovative media-based project, which involves learners engaging meaningfully with language through engagement with their local context.

Film scripts

Daily Script – *http://www.dailyscript.com/*
An extensive collection of free, downloadable movie scripts and screenplays.

Drew's Scrip-o-rama –
http://www.script-o-rama.com/snazzy/dircut.html
An index of over 10,000 film and television scripts available on the internet.

Animated movie makers

Go Animate – *http://goanimate.com/*
A site where learners create their own animated short films.

Zimmer Twins – *http://www.zimmertwins.com/*
Learners can create short animated clips, add subtitles and voice-overs.

Subtitling and revoicing

Bombay TV – *http://www.grapheine.com/bombaytv/*
A fun site where learners can add subtitles and voice-overs to television and film clips.

ClipFlair – *http://clipflair.net/*
A site where learners can revoice and caption video clips.

Recommended reading

The Age of the Image: Redefining Literacy in a World of Screens by Stephen Apkon (Farrar, Straus and Giroux 2013)
A twenty-first-century masterpiece on the play of word and image in our present culture, and on how to communicate effectively 'in a world of screens'. The chapter *Teaching a New Generation* is required reading for any educator.

Literacy in the New Media Age by Gunther Kress (Routledge 2003)
A seminal work on the changing nature of literacy in the twenty-first century.

Understanding Movies by Louis Giannetti (Prentice Hall 2002)
An essential text for anyone interested in becoming more film literate.

How to Read a Film: Movies, Media, and Beyond by James Monaco (OUP 2009)
A classic text for anyone interested in knowing how to understand a film.

English Teaching and the Moving Image by Andrew Goodwyn (Routledge 2004)
A practical and straightforward guide to teaching about the moving image.

Using Authentic Video in the Language Classroom by Jane Sherman (CUP 2003)
An outstanding methodology book, which guides and supports teachers with practical suggestions for activities designed round moving images.

Film by Susan Stempleski and Barry Tomalin (OUP 2001)
A highly practical book, which helps teachers select, structure and teach lessons around film.

The Director in the Classroom: How Filmmaking Inspires Learning by Nikos Theodosakis (Tech4Learning 2001)
An excellent film production handbook for teachers.

Language Learning with Digital Video
by Ben Goldstein and Paul Driver (CUP 2014)
A practical resource book for teachers interested in using digital video in the language classroom.

Bringing Online Video into the Classroom
by Jamie Keddie (OUP 2014)
A guide to using online video creatively in the classroom.

References

[1] Bazalgette, C *Impacts of Moving Image Education: A Summary of Research* Scottish Screen 2009

[2] Apkon, S *The Age of the Image: Redefining Literacy in a World of Screens* Farrar, Straus and Giroux 2013

[3] 'Story of the movies – Mr. Smith goes to Washington: Teacher's guide' *http://www.storyofmovies.org/ common/11041/pdfs/msgtw/msgtw_tg_intro.pdf*

[4] Chan, D and Herrero, C *Using Film to Teach Languages: A Teacher's Toolkit* Cornerhouse Education 2010

[5] Thoman, E and Jolls, T 'Five Questions That Can Change the World' *Center for Media Literacy* 2005

[6] Apkon, S op. cit.

[7] '21st Century Literacy: A strategy for film education across the UK' British Film Institute 2011 *http://www.culturallearningalliance.org.uk/userfiles/ files/2010/02/FilmLiteracyLoRes.pdf*

[8] Goodwyn, A *English Teaching and the Moving Image* Routledge 2004

[9] Apkon, S op. cit.

[10] '21st Century Literacy: A strategy for film education across the UK' op. cit.

[11] Wenders, W quoted in 'The Beauty of a Second' 2012 *https://vimeo.com/31604545*

[12] Goodwyn, A op. cit.

[13] Mackey, M 'Popular culture and sophisticated reading: Men in black' *English in Education* 1999

[14] Blau, A 'The Future of Independent Media' *Deeper News* 10 (1) 2005 *http://www.namac.org/deep-focus-report*

[15] Jenkins, H et al 'Confronting the Challenges of Participatory Culture: Media Education for the 21st Century' 2009 *http://www.newmedialiteracies.org/ wp-content/uploads/pdfs/NMLWhitePaper.pdf*

[16] Monaco, J *How to Read a Film: Movies, Media, and Beyond* OUP 2009

[17] Goodwyn, A op. cit.

[18] Apkon, S op. cit.

[19] Kress, G *Literacy in the New Media Age* Routledge 2003

[20] Kress, G ibid.

[21] Goodwyn, A op. cit.

[22] Jewitt, C 'The Visual in Learning and Creativity London: Creative Partnerships' 2008 *http://www.mirandanet.ac.uk/ vl_blog/wp-content/uploads/2009/02/the-visual-in-learning -andcreativity-168.pdf*

[23] 'The New London Group: A Pedagogy of Multiliteracies: Designing Social Futures' *Harvard Educational Review* 66 (1) *1996 http://wwwstatic.kern.org/filer/ blogWrite44ManilaWebsite/paul/articles/A_Pedagogy_of_ Multiliteracies_Designing_Social_Futures.htm*

[24] Goodwyn, A op. cit.

[25] Kress, G op. cit.

[26] 'Reframing Literacy: British Film Institute Report' *http://www.bfi.org.uk/sites/bfi.org.uk/files/downloads/ bfi-education-reframing-literacy-2013-04.pdf*

[27] Jewitt, C op. cit.

[28] '21st Century Literacy: A strategy for film education across the UK' op. cit.

[29] Media Literacy Centre *http://www.medialit.org/ media-literacy-definition-and-more*

[30] 'Screening Literacy: Executive Report' European Commission 2013 *http://edition.pagesuite-professional. co.uk//launch.aspx?pbid=25c57922-2908-45b5-b752- e891849e520f*

[31] Jenkins, H et al 'Confronting the Challenges of Participatory Culture: Media Education for the 21st Century' op. cit.

[32] Scorcese, M 'Acquiring Visual Literacy' *Edutopia* 2006 *http://www.edutopia.org/martin-scorsese-teaching-visual- literacy*

[33] Giannetti, L *Understanding Movies* Prentice Hall 2002

[34] Culkin, J *Film Study in the High School: An Analysis and Rationale* Harvard Graduate School of Education 1964

[35] Lucas, G 'Life on the Screen' *Edutopia, The George Lucas Educational Foundation* 2004 *http://www.edutopia.org/life-screen*

[36] Kress, G op. cit.

[37] Apkon, S op. cit.

[38] Lessig, L quoted in 'Remix Culture' *Stanford Social Innovation Opinion Blog* 2009 *http://csi.gsb.stanford.edu/remix-culture*

[39] Jenkins, H and Kelley, W *Reading in a Participatory Culture: Remixing Moby-Dick in the English Classroom* Teachers College Press and National Writing Project 2013

[40] Jenkins, H 'Participatory Culture and Media Education' *Edutopia* 2013 *http://www.edutopia.org/henry-jenkins- participatory-culture-video*

41 Jenkins, H 'Participatory Culture and Media Education' ibid.

42 Jenkins, H et al 'Confronting the Challenges of Participatory Culture: Media Education for the 21st Century' op. cit.

43 Brannagh, K quoted in 'Film: 21st Century Literacy – Showreel' 2012 *https://www.youtube.com/watch?v=OLVfa53PfPA*

44 Apkon, S op. cit.

45 Lucas, G op. cit.

46 Jewitt, C op. cit.

47 Apkon, S op. cit.

48 Brannagh, K op. cit.

49 *Charter for Media Literacy* UK Film Council 2005

50 Goodwyn, A op. cit.

51 Jewitt, C op. cit.

52 Theodosakis, N *The Director in the Classroom: How Filmmaking Inspires Learning* Tech4Learning 2001

53 Edison, T quoted in Apkon, S op. cit.

54 Goodwyn, A op. cit.

55 Goodwyn, A ibid.

56 Edison, T quoted in Apkon, S op. cit.

57 Cruse, E 'Using educational video in the classroom: Theory, Research and Practice' 2006 *http://www.libraryvideo.com/articles/article26.asp*

58 'Study of School Uses of Television and Video 1996–1997: School Year Summary Report' Corporation for Public Broadcasting 1997

59 Hobbs, R 'Non-optimal use of video in the classroom' *Learning, Media and Technology* 31 (1) March 2006 *http://mediaeducationlab.com/pub/non-optimal-uses-video-classroom*

60 Goodwyn, A op. cit.

61 Cruse, E op. cit.

62 'Integrating Film into Education – Advocacy Report' British Film Institute 2012 *http://www.independentcinemaoffice.org.uk/media/Misc/film-21st-century-literacy-advocacy-report.pdf*

63 Stafford, T *Teaching Visual Literacy in the Primary Classroom: Comic Books, Film, Television and Picture Narratives* David Fulton Books 2010

64 Kidron, B 'The Shared Wonder of Film' 2012 *http://www.ted.com/talks/beeban_kidron_the_shared_wonder_of_film/transcript*

65 Chan, D and Herrero, C op. cit.

66 'Integrating Film into Education – Advocacy Report' op. cit.

67 Reid, M quoted in 'Film: 21st Century Literacy – Showreel' 2012 *https://www.youtube.com/watch?v=OLVfa53PfPA*

68 Buckingham, D 'Making it Explicit: Towards a Theory of Media Learning' in Buckingham, D (Ed) *Watching Media Learning* Falmer Press 1990

69 British Film Institute 'Using Film in the Classroom: A Practical Guide' 2010 *http://mediaedwales.org.uk/pdf/usingfilm.pdf*

70 Robinson, M *Children Reading Print and Television* Falmer Press 1997

71 Rushdie, S *Step Across This Line: Collected Nonfiction 1992–2002* Modern Library Paperbacks 2003

72 Vetrie, M 'Using Film to Improve Literacy Skills' 2004 *http://michaelvetrie.com/usingfilm.pdf*

73 Theodosakis, N op. cit.

74 Apkon, S op. cit.

75 Jewitt, C op. cit.

76 Lenhardt, A and Madden, M 'Teens Content Creators and Consumers' Pew Internet and American Life Project 2005 *http://www.pewinternet.org/files/oldmedia/Files/Reports/2005/PIP_Teens_Content_Creation.pdf.pdf*

77 Hobbs, R op. cit.

78 Chan, D and Herrero, C op. cit.

79 Whitcher, A *Uncover: Teacher's Book* CUP 2015

80 Goodwyn, A op. cit.

81 Goldstein, B and Driver, P *Language learning with Digital Video* CUP 2014

82 Littlewood, W *Communicative Language Teaching: An Introduction* CUP 1981

83 Krashen, S D *The Input Hypothesis: Issues and Implications* Longman 1985

84 'Common European Framework of Reference for Languages' Council of Europe 2001 *http://www.coe.int/t/dg4/linguistic/Source/Framework_EN.pdf*

85 Maley, A op. cit.

86 Sherman, J *Using Authentic Video in the Language Classroom* CUP 2003

87 Mohanty, S 'Technology in Language Classrooms: Filmmaking as a Tool for Developing Life Skills' *Global Perspectives, Local Initiatives* 2011 *http://www.nus.edu.sg/celc/research/books/3rdsymposium/097to106-seemita.pdf*

88 Maley, A op. cit.

89 'Common European Framework of Reference for Languages' op. cit.

90 Chan, D and Herrero, C op. cit.

91 Chan, D and Herrero, C ibid.

92 Goldstein, B and Driver, P op. cit.

93 Whitcher, A *Uncover: Teacher's Book* op. cit.

94 Lucas, G op. cit.

Film in Action has so far argued on behalf of using film in the language classroom and beyond. We are now ready to turn our attention to some practical activities that you can carry out with your learners.

In Chapter One, there is an emphasis on encouraging the learners to actively watch and engage with a wide variety of moving image texts, and improve their language skills while at the same time developing their visual literacy.

In Chapter Two, the emphasis is on the learners actively producing their own short films and videos, and all the activities have the common aim of promoting language learning and the development of communicative competence.

Chapter One
Watching actively

Chapter One presents a wide range of activities which will help *you* exploit moving images in your classes. And all of the activities have the common aim of helping *your learners* improve their knowledge and use of English, covering all four language skills.

There is an emphasis on developing a critical 'film literacy' through the medium of English. In other words:

- Helping your learners analyse and interpret moving images.
- Encouraging them to think critically about film itself.
- Looking beyond the surface of the screen, to consider a film's intentions and techniques.

The learners will acquire some necessary specialist vocabulary relating to moving images, which will help them analyse carefully moving image conventions and techniques.

The aim is to help learners understand that sound and image convey narrative information in different ways – focusing on how sound presents information in film, and using visual clues as a springboard for a wide variety of both oral and written communication tasks, which will help unlock your learners' speaking and writing skills.

Setting the scene

To invite the learners to reflect on how they 'read' a film.

Pre-production

Make sufficient copies of a template like the one opposite, and choose a film clip of between four and six minutes.

Teachers who don't have time to source films for themselves will find a link to a suitable film clip here: *http://bit.ly/KmGUAf*

Action!

- ☐ Write *Passively watching a film* and *Actively watching a film* on the board, and ask the learners if they know the difference between them. Invite them to discuss the questions, but don't give a definitive answer.

- ☐ Tell the learners they are going to watch a short film clip and complete a worksheet which may help them understand the difference.

- ☐ Distribute the worksheet and go through the vocabulary, to make sure the learners understand it.

- ☐ Play your clip two or three times:
  - ☐ Pause after each viewing, to give the learners time to make notes.

- ☐ In groups of three or four, they compare their answers.

- ☐ Conduct a feedback session:
  - ☐ Go through the worksheet, to discuss the responses.

- ☐ Go back to the phrases on the board: *Passively watching a film* and *Actively watching a film*. Ask the learners if they are now able to tell the difference between the two ways of viewing a film. Try to elicit:
  - ☐ *Passively watching a film* means viewing it in a non-critical manner.
  - ☐ *Actively watching a film* means trying to understand the aesthetics of film production, treating the film as a visual text and learning how to read and decode it, and thinking critically about film as a visual medium.

- ☐ Hold a plenary session based on the following questions:
  - ☐ *Do the learners normally watch a film actively or passively?*
  - ☐ *What are the advantages and disadvantages of each?*

Post-production

For homework, you can ask the learners to analyse one of their favourite film scenes as 'active viewers'.

Acknowledgement

This activity is adapted from an activity in *Using Film to Teach Languages: A Teacher's Toolkit* by Carmen Herrero and Deborah Chan (Cornerhouse Education).

Genre	
Plot and themes	
Settings (inside/outside)	
Use of camera (camera shots/movements)	
Lighting and colour	
Sound and music	
Costume	
Props	
Acting/performance	
Spoken language (formality/register)	
Facial expression and body language	

Note: It will be useful to make sure the learners know the names of the various accepted film genres:

- ☐ *Comedy*
- ☐ *Romantic comedy (romcom)*
- ☐ *Romance*
- ☐ *Thriller*
- ☐ *Psychological thriller*
- ☐ *Horror*
- ☐ *Science fiction (Sci-Fi)*
- ☐ *Drama*
- ☐ *Historical drama*
- ☐ *Costume drama*
- ☐ *Adventure*
- ☐ *Fantasy*
- ☐ *Western*

We will be exploring *new* film genres in the final section of this chapter, starting on page 68.

Three Ss and three Cs

To analyse a film clip, generating discussion
on the multi-faceted nature of film.

Pre-production

Choose a film clip which takes place in one setting and has
interaction between two or more characters. Prepare at least
three questions for each of the areas you are going to discuss,
as in the example opposite.

Teachers who don't have time to source films for themselves
will find a link to a suitable film clip here:
http://bit.ly/19z4Axi

Action!

☐ Write the alliterations *Story*, *Setting* and *Sound* and
Characters, *Colour* and *Camera* on the board, and ask the
learners to write them down.

☐ Explain that you are going to show a short film clip,
and that you want them to make notes in each category
on what they see and hear.

☐ Go through each category, and give three questions you
would like the learners to think about as they watch.

☐ Play the film.

☐ Give the learners a few minutes to complete their notes:
   ☐ When they are ready, pair them and ask them to
   compare their notes.

☐ Play the film again.

☐ Hold a plenary discussion on each of the categories.

Post-production

For homework, you can ask the learners to write a
composition, analysing the scene you showed.

Alternatively, the learners choose a scene from one of their
favourite films and analyse it, using the three Ss and three Cs.
They write a composition, or download the film and do a
voice-over analysing it (see *Voice-over* on page 54).

Story:

☐ *What story does the film tell?*

☐ *What happened before this scene?*

☐ *What's going to happen after this scene?*

Setting:

☐ *Where does the action take place?*

☐ *How quickly can we establish where the story
takes place?*

☐ *Does the setting lead to certain expectations?*

Sound:

☐ *Is there any music?*

☐ *Does the music create an atmosphere?*

☐ *How do the characters speak?*

Characters:

☐ *What do we learn about the characters through
what they say?*

☐ *What do we learn about the characters through
what they do?*

☐ *What do we learn about the characters through
visual clues?*

Colour:

☐ *What colours are used in this scene?*

☐ *Are the colours warm or cold?*

☐ *How do the colours make you feel?*

Camera:

☐ *Note down any close-up, medium and wide shots
in the scene. Why were these shots used?*

☐ *If there are any close-up shots, what emotions
do they represent?*

☐ *Can you think of any adjectives or phrases to
describe these emotions?*

Note: There is more information on camera shots in the next
activity on page 35.

Camera shots

To discuss the conventions and techniques
of the craft of film making.

Pre-production

Find examples of a *wide shot*, *medium shot* and *close-up shot*:

☐ Use either film stills or screenshots of films.

☐ Prepare a definition of each type of shot, such as the ones opposite.

☐ Find a film clip in which there are clear examples of wide shots, medium shots and close-up shots.

Teachers who don't have time to source films for themselves will find a link to a suitable film clip here: *http://bit.ly/1cKWwZh*

Action!

☐ Show the learners the wide shot, the medium shot and the close-up shot which you have selected.

☐ Elicit or give the name and a definition of each one:
  ☐ It will probably be necessary to supply the names *and* the definitions.

☐ Tell the learners they are going to watch a film clip in which they will see examples of each type of shot:
  ☐ As they watch, their task is to note down examples of each type of shot.

☐ Show the film clip.

☐ Ask the learners to compare their notes with a partner.

☐ Show the film a second time:
  ☐ As they watch, their task now is to tell you to pause when they see examples of each type of shot.

☐ Each time, ask them to discuss why *that* type of shot was chosen for *that* moment in the film.

Post-production

For homework, the learners can watch one of their favourite film scenes:

☐ They note down examples of each type of shot, and why it was used.

☐ In the following lesson, they show their clips, pause when a type of shot appears and explain why it is used for that moment in the film.

Alternatively, they can capture examples of long, medium and close-up shots on their mobile phones:

☐ They send you the image files.

☐ You create a *PowerPoint* presentation of the images.

In the following lesson, you show the presentation, for the learners to identify their specific shots and explain them.

Wide shot

A shot of a broad field of action, taken with a wide-angle lens.

Wide shots are often 'establishing' shots – used to show the whole setting of a scene, and help the audience understand what is happening.

Medium shot

Medium shots show one or more characters from the waist or knees up, sharing actions or dialogues that are key to the narrative.

Their main purpose is to move the action along.

Close-up shot

A close-up shot is a frame filled with just one (usually small) part of a character or object.

It is often used to emphasise the expression on a character's face or detailed features of an object.

Note: There is more information on 'establishing shots' in the next activity on page 36.

Establishing shots

To write the opening paragraph of a novel,
starting with a film.

Pre-production

Find an example of an 'establishing shot' – a shot which
shows the whole setting of a scene – at the start of a film.

These are some films which have interesting opening
establishing shots:
Breakfast at Tiffany's
To Kill a Mockingbird
Saving Private Ryan
Vertigo
Psycho
American Beauty

Teachers who don't have time to source films for themselves
will find a link to a suitable film clip here:
http://bit.ly/1hJGYoh

Action!

☐ Show the learners your establishing shot:
   ▫ Elicit or explain that establishing shots are used to
     show the whole setting of a scene in a similar way to
     how an author describes the setting in detail at the start
     of a novel.

☐ Invite the learners to say everything they can see in the
   establishing shot:
   ▫ You write the words on the board.

☐ Tell them that they are authors writing the first paragraph
   of a novel, and that they have to portray the same
   information:
   ▫ You set a time limit of 15 minutes.
   ▫ You walk round, providing help with language as
     necessary.

☐ When the learners have finished their paragraphs, ask
   them to read them to another learner.

☐ Invite them to read out their paragraphs to the class.

☐ Now show the first scene of the film, and ask the learners
   to compare their written descriptions with what they see
   on the screen.

Post-production

For homework, the learners can write the *second* scene of
the film.

Alternatively, they choose the opening scene of one of *their*
favourite films and imagine they are an author writing
the first paragraph of a novel. Their task is to portray the
opening scene as a written text.

Opening titles

To look at the lexis relating to film conventions
and techniques.

Pre-production

Select an interesting opening title sequence. Hundreds of
beautiful examples can be found at Art of the Title:
http://www.artofthetitle.com/

Action!

☐ Write *Opening title sequence* on the board:
   ▫ Elicit or explain that this is the method by which films
     present their title, cast members, director and key
     members of the production team at the beginning
     (or the end) of a film.

☐ Write the following words on the board:
   ▫ Film studio   ▫ Director of photography
   ▫ Producer   ▫ Editor
   ▫ Executive producer   ▫ Costume designer
   ▫ Director   ▫ Screenwriter

☐ Go through the vocabulary with the learners.

☐ Tell the learners they are going to watch the opening title
   sequence of a film:
   ▫ Their task is to identify the title, the film studio,
     main actors, director and other key members of the
     production team.

☐ Show the title sequence.

☐ Pair the learners, and ask them to compare their answers.

☐ Show the title sequence again:
   ▫ You pause each time a credit appears.
   ▫ You elicit or explain the role of each person.

☐ Divide the class into groups of three or four and set a
   time limit of 10 minutes:
   ▫ *What do they think the film's genre is?*
   ▫ *Who do they think the intended audience is?*
   ▫ *Can they predict the film's content or message?*

☐ Hold a feedback session on the learners' answers.

☐ Read out a synopsis of the film, and ask the learners if
   their answers were correct. Alternatively, show the first
   scene of the film.

Post-production

For homework, you can ask the learners to choose one of
their favourite films or television series, watch the opening
title sequence and identify the main actors, director,
producer and other key members of the production team.

Trailer talk

To reflect on and compare the conventions of film trailers.

Pre-production

Prepare a list of film trailer conventions to give or dictate to your learners. See opposite.

Find a film trailer website, such as:

- Yahoo Movies
  http://movies.yahoo.com
- Apple Trailers
  http://apple.com/trailers/
- Coming Soon
  http://www.comingsoon.net/trailers/

Choose a typical trailer which has lots of the conventions in your list. Also, find an unusual trailer which does *not* have many of the conventions.

For teachers who don't have time to source films themselves, here are links to two suitable film trailers:
http://bit.ly/1cJJ0aG
http://bit.ly/Nhp2Im

Action!

- ☐ Write the word *Trailer* on the board:
  - ☐ Elicit or explain that a trailer is a short advertisement for a feature-length film.
  - ☐ Ask the learners what you usually see and hear in a trailer.

- ☐ Give them your list of film trailer conventions, and explain that they are common features of a trailer:
  - ☐ Ask the learners to read the list, and clarify any doubts they may have.

- ☐ Tell them they are going to watch a trailer:
  - ☐ As they watch, their task is to identify which of the conventions appear.

- ☐ Show the trailer.

- ☐ Divide the class into small groups, to compare their answers, then get feedback from the whole class.

- ☐ Tell the learners you are going to show the trailer again:
  - ☐ They tell you to pause every time one of the conventions appears.
  - ☐ You discuss each convention as it appears.

- ☐ Now tell the learners that not all film trailers are the same, and that they are going to see an *unusual* trailer:
  - ☐ As they watch, their task is to notice which conventions do *not* appear.

- ☐ Show the trailer.

- ☐ The opening establishes setting and characters.
- ☐ A build-up develops characters.
- ☐ A dilemma, or series of complications the characters are faced with, is revealed.
- ☐ Events related to how the characters try to overcome the obstacles are shown.
- ☐ A voice-over tells the story of the film.
- ☐ The voice-over is a deep male voice.
- ☐ Information about the stars is given.
- ☐ Information about the director is given.
- ☐ Graphics are superimposed.
- ☐ Lines of dialogue are heard.
- ☐ Music creates atmosphere.
- ☐ Dramatic camera angles are chosen to show events and characters.
- ☐ The trailer ends in a climax to 'tease' the audience.
- ☐ The title of the film is placed at the end of the trailer.

- ☐ Get the learners to compare their answers in their groups.
- ☐ Hold a plenary session based on the following questions:
  - ☐ *How was the second trailer different from the first?*
  - ☐ *Which of the two trailers has a greater impact?*
  - ☐ *Which of the films would they prefer to see? Why?*

Post-production

You can give the learners the address of one of the film trailer sites. For homework, they choose three trailers of films currently showing at the cinema:

- ☐ They watch all three trailers and decide which film they would most like to watch.
- ☐ They write a composition explaining their choice.

Alternatively, the learners find the trailer of their favourite movie, watch it at home and, in class, discuss whether it does the film justice:

- ☐ *Does it cover all of the main elements?*
- ☐ *What's missing?*
- ☐ *Does it give too much away?*

Deconstructing an ad

To debate the conventions and aesthetics
of TV advertisements.

Pre-production

Select a variety of very short TV ads that you think your
learners will find interesting.

There are many websites, such as iSpot.tv, dedicated
exclusively to TV adverts (*http://www.ispot.tv/browse*).

Action!

☐ Divide the class into groups of three or four.

☐ Tell the learners they are going to watch a selection of
short TV ads:
  ◦ After watching, each group is going to have to decide
  which they like most.

☐ Show the ads.

☐ In their groups, the learners discuss the various strategies
used by the advertiser to influence the audience.

☐ They each make a chart to communicate their findings,
including examples of the following:
  ◦ Stated and implied information
  ◦ Persuasive language
  ◦ Interesting words and phrases
  ◦ Powerful visuals

☐ Each group then presents their findings to another group.

☐ Conduct a feedback session with all the learners, based on
their findings.

Post-production

For homework, you can ask the learners to choose another
ad they like, and to write a composition – deconstructing it,
as they did in the lesson.

Alternatively, you ask them to plan their own film ads, using
the persuasive techniques they examined in class.

What's next?

To make predictions about what is going to
happen next in a film.

Pre-production

Select a short film with little or no dialogue, but which has
clear discernable actions.

Teachers who don't have time to source films for themselves
will find a link to a suitable short film here:
http://bit.ly/1dfTngq

Action!

☐ Tell the learners they are going to watch a short film,
and that you are going to pause the film at a key point:
  ◦ They have to predict what is going to happen next.
  ◦ They have to support their predictions.

☐ Show the film, pausing at a suspenseful point.

☐ Pair the learners, to discuss:
  ◦ *What do they think is going to happen next?*
  ◦ *Why?*

☐ Restart the film, pausing at another suspenseful point:
  ◦ *Were their predictions accurate?*
  ◦ *What do they think is going to happen next?*
  ◦ *Why?*

☐ Show the rest of the film:
  ◦ *Were their predictions accurate?*

Post-production

For homework, the learners can write the story of the film
and continue the story after the film ends.

Encourage them to use the skill of predicting, *whenever*
they watch a film.

You can find an example of this activity here:
http://bit.ly/1i0XqBL

Memory game

To focus on visual details, to increase
general understanding of a story.

Pre-production

Select a short silent film or film clip.

Teachers who don't have time to source films for themselves
will find a link to a suitable short film here:
http://bit.ly/19NqmuS

Action!

☐ Pair the learners.

☐ Tell them what their task is:
  ☐ To watch a short film or film clip.
  ☐ To write down as many visual details as they can
    remember.
  ☐ To compare their list with their partner.

☐ Play the film.

☐ Each pair then makes a list of all the visual details they
  can remember.

☐ Set a time limit of five minutes, before inviting the pairs
  to compare their list with another pair.

☐ Play the film again.

☐ Ask the learners to tell you to pause when you come to
  a visual detail they have noted down.

Post-production

The learners can write a narrative, describing the story told
in the short film.

Alternatively, after viewing the film, the learners write down
three questions about visual details in the clip. For example:
  ☐ *What was the weather like?*
  ☐ *Who saw the tiger first?*
  ☐ *How many animals where there?*

They ask the others their questions.

Acknowledgement

This activity is adapted from an activity in *Film* by Susan
Stempleski and Barry Tomalin (Oxford University Press).

10 words

To focus on visual details in a film – and revise items of
vocabulary at the same time.

Pre-production

Select a short film or clip which shows things which are
items of vocabulary you have studied recently with your
class:
  ☐ Watch the film and note down 10 such items.
  ☐ Add 10 other related words which you have also studied
    recently, but which do not appear in the film.
  ☐ Jumble the 20 words.

Action!

☐ Dictate the 20 words to the learners.

☐ Tell them that they are going to watch a film in which
  some, but not all, of the vocabulary items appear.

☐ As they watch, their task is to tick the items which
  they see.

☐ Show the film.

☐ Pair the learners, to compare their answers.

☐ Show the film again.

☐ As they watch, their task is to tell you to pause the film,
  every time they see one of the items.

Post-production

For homework, the learners can write a short composition
or dialogue in which they incorporate the 10 items of
vocabulary that appear in the film.

Ordering the objects

To identify and sequence items of vocabulary
as they appear in a film.

Pre-production

Select a short film or clip which shows things which are
items of vocabulary you have studied recently with your
class. Watch the film and note down 10 items.

Teachers who don't have time to source films for themselves
will find a link to a suitable short film here:
http://bit.ly/1dBxUhy

Action!

☐ Dictate your 10 words to the learners.

☐ Tell them that they are going to watch a film in which all
of the vocabulary items appear.

☐ As they watch, their task is to number the items in the
order they appear.

☐ Show the film.

☐ Pair the learners, to compare their answers.

☐ Ask them to write a short composition:
  ☐ They incorporate the 10 items of vocabulary in the
  film.
  ☐ You set a time limit of ten minutes.

☐ Pair the learners, and ask them to read their composition
to their partner.

☐ Finally, they read their compositions to the rest of the
class.

Post-production

For homework, you can ask the learners to find a film clip,
short film or film which contains items of vocabulary which
you have studied recently:

☐ They watch the film and note down 10 items.
☐ In the following lesson, a learner dictates their 10 items
of vocabulary to the class.
☐ The others watch the film and put the items in the order
they appear.

In subsequent lessons, you ask other learners to follow the
same procedure.

Ordering the actions

To work together, sequencing events
in a short film or scene.

Pre-production

Select a short film or scene which has a lot of different
actions:

☐ Prepare 10 statements about the action in the scene.
☐ Jumble them up, to ensure they are not in chronological
order.
☐ Cut the paper into strips, so that each strip has a sentence
on it.

Teachers who don't have time to source films for themselves
will find a link to a suitable film clip here:
http://bit.ly/1ixdmMu

Action!

☐ Pair the learners, and give each pair a set of paper strips.

☐ Tell them they are going to watch a short film or scene
in which they will see 10 actions corresponding to the
statements, such as:
  ☐ *The man knocks on the door.*
  ☐ *The man parks his car.*

☐ Their task is to put the statements in chronological order.

☐ Show the film twice.

☐ Pair the learners, and give them five minutes to sequence
the statements correctly.

☐ Show the film again, checking the sequencing.

Post-production

For homework, the learners can go to YouTube and choose a
scene from a film which has a lot of different actions:

☐ They prepare five statements about actions in the scene
and jumble them, to ensure they are not in chronological
order.
☐ In the next lesson, each learner writes their five statements
on the board, or dictates them to the other learners.
☐ The learner shows the film scene they have chosen.
☐ The others have to put the actions in chronological order.

Acknowledgement

This activity is adapted from an activity in *Using Authentic
Film in the Language Classroom* by Jane Sherman
(Cambridge University Press).

Ordering the scenes

To show three short scenes, for the learners to put them in the correct order.

Pre-production

Select three scenes from the DVD menu of a film. Make sure there are scenes *before* the first and the third.

Action!

☐ Tell the learners they are going to watch three short scenes from a film – in an *incorrect* order:
- ◌ *Which scene comes first?*
- ◌ *Which comes second?*
- ◌ *Which comes third?*

☐ Show the three scenes in the *incorrect* order.

☐ Pair the learners, to put the scenes in the correct order and give reasons for their answers:
- ◌ Elicit the correct order and the reasons.

☐ Show the three scenes in the *correct* order, so the learners can compare the sequence with their answers.

☐ Pair the learners again, to predict what happened before the *first* scene:
- ◌ They write a short narrative, explaining the scene they imagine.
- ◌ You set a time limit of five minutes.

☐ Each pair of learners explains their narrative to another pair.

☐ Show that scene from the film, for the learners to compare *their* narratives with what they see and hear in the actual film.

☐ Repeat this procedure with new pairs – the learners start by predicting what happened before the *third* scene.

☐ If you have time, show all five scenes.

Post-production

For homework, you can ask the learners to write a narrative describing the events they saw in the five scenes.

Make it your own!

To encourage the learners to respond personally to a visual text.

Pre-production

Select a short film or clip.

Teachers who don't have time to source films for themselves will find a link to a suitable short film here: *http://bit.ly/19zmTCA*

Prepare some sentence stems, such as:
- ◌ *I liked …*
- ◌ *It reminded me of …*
- ◌ *I felt confused/excited/surprised/unhappy/frightened when …*

Action!

☐ Tell the learners that they are going to watch a short film or clip.

☐ Dictate your sentence stems, or write them up on the board and ask the learners to copy them.

☐ Play the film:
- ◌ The learners respond personally to the text.
- ◌ They will complete the sentence stems in a way which is true for *them*.

☐ Give the learners a time limit of three minutes to complete their sentences.

☐ Put them into groups of three or four, to compare their responses.

☐ Conduct a feedback session with the whole class, based on the responses.

Post-production

For homework, the learners can write a paragraph about how the short film made them feel.

You can find an example of this activity here: *http://bit.ly/1jVMqZM*

Three question types

To encourage the learners to gain ownership
of a visual text – by asking questions.

Pre-production

Prepare three types of questions about a film the learners
have seen recently. Opposite are examples of three question
types, with sample questions, about *Romeo and Juliet*.

Action!

☐ Dictate or show the learners the questions you have
prepared about a film they have watched recently.

☐ Point out that there are three types of questions, and try
to elicit the following answers:
  ▫ *Questions of fact* can be answered with a word, phrase
  or visual detail from the film.
  ▫ *Questions of interpretation* can be answered only by
  interpreting the facts given in, or suggested by, the film.
  ▫ *Questions beyond the text* cannot be answered by
  looking within this single film, but by examining
  society and the world at large.

☐ Tell the learners that they are going to watch a short
film clip. However, you are not going to ask them any
questions about it:
  ▫ They should write *their own questions* about the film.
  ▫ They should write two questions for each of the three
  types of questions you have looked at.

☐ Show the film clip two or three times.

☐ Invite the learners to write their six questions individually:
  ▫ You set a time limit of 10 minutes.
  ▫ You walk round, providing help with language as
  necessary.

☐ Put the learners into pairs, to ask and answer each other's
questions.

☐ Hold a plenary discussion, based on their questions.

Post-production

For homework, the learners can choose a scene from one
of their favourite films. They write six questions about the
scene:
  ▫ They write two questions for each of the three types of
  questions you have looked at in class.
  ▫ They answer their own questions.

Alternatively, you show a film clip or short film – and they
follow the same procedure at home.

Acknowledgement

This activity is adapted from an activity in *Reading in the
Dark: Using Film as a Tool in the English Classroom* by
John Golden (National Council of Teachers of English).

Questions of fact

Who is Romeo in love with at first?

Who are the two feuding families?

Questions of interpretation

What makes Romeo fall in love with Juliet so quickly?

What will Romeo have to do in order to win Juliet?

Questions beyond the text

*Why is the relationship between parents and children
difficult?*

What does 'real love' mean?

Five Ws and an H

To find out information about a film – by asking questions using the five Ws and an H.

Pre-production

Select a film clip of a scene with a lot of dramatic action.

Teachers who don't have time to source films for themselves will find a link to a suitable film clip here:
http://bit.ly/1hctlBP

Action!

☐ Ask the learners what information they want to find out when they read or watch a news item.

☐ Elicit the question words *Who, What, Where, When, Why* and *How* – the five Ws and an H – and write them on the board.

☐ Tell the learners that these are questions asked by journalists to provide the basic information about a news story. Write up examples:
  - **Who** *is it about?*
  - **What** *happened?*
  - **Where** *did it happen?*
  - **When** *did it happen?*
  - **Why** *did it happen?*
  - **How** *did it happen?*

☐ Tell the learners they are going to watch a film clip which shows an event which could be reported in a newspaper.

☐ Their task is to imagine they are journalists writing a news item about it, answering 'the five Ws and an H':
  - The first time they watch the clip, they try to get a general idea of what happens but do not write anything down.
  - The second time they watch, they make brief notes to answer the five Ws and an H.

☐ Show the film twice.

☐ When the learners have completed their notes, ask them to compare them with a partner.

☐ Hold a plenary discussion based on the six questions listed above.

Post-production

For homework, the learners can write a short news story based on the film clip in which they answer the six questions.

Alternatively, they read the script aloud several times and then make a film of themselves reporting the news item:
  - They send you the film file.
  - You watch the film and give feedback on content, presentation and pronunciation.

In subsequent lessons, show the films to the class and ask the learners to comment on them. Ensure that they have addressed the questions and managed to answer all six.

Under observation

To write observation questions about a silent film.

Pre-production

Select a short film or clip which has no, or very little, dialogue.

Teachers who don't have time to source films for themselves will find a link to a suitable short film here:
http://bit.ly/1kf51Bl

Action!

☐ Tell the learners they are going to watch a short film or clip which has little or no dialogue:
  - As they watch, their task will be to focus on the visual elements – and to try to remember as much as possible.

☐ Show the film.

☐ Divide the class into groups of three or four, to write 10 'observation questions' about the film. For example:
  - *What colour is the shirt the boy is wearing?*

☐ Set a time limit of 10 minutes and walk round, providing help with language as necessary.

☐ Pair the learners with a member of another group:
  - They ask each other their observation questions.

☐ Show the film again.

☐ Ask the learners to check the answers to their questions.

Post-production

The learners can write down the sequence of events in a short film, jumble them and then ask a partner to put them in the correct order.

A moving poem

To visualise and describe mental imagery.

Pre-production

Select a short film which is a visual poem.

Excellent examples can be found at Moving Poems:
http://movingpoems.com

Transcribe the poem for the learners, and make copies.

For teachers who don't have time to source films themselves, here is a link to a suitable poem video:
http://bit.ly/1qeRRoP

Action!

☐ Read the poem to the learners, or play the video with sound only.

☐ Ask the learners to discuss the following questions:
-    *Do they recognise the poem?*
-    *What is the theme?*
-    *What is the main emotion of the poem?*

☐ Distribute the poem.

☐ Put the learners into small groups, to read the poem and visualise images which might appear in an accompanying video.

☐ The groups explain their images to another group.

☐ Show the film.

☐ The learners discuss the following questions:
-    *Are the images similar to what they visualised?*
-    *How do the images connect with the words?*
-    *Do the images enhance the words? How?*

Post-production

The learners can dub their voice-over onto the original.

This activity can also be used with music videos and song lyrics.

Visual poetry on page 91 is an excellent activity to follow on from this one.

That's so typical!

To identify stereotypes in film.

Pre-production

Select a film clip which has a clear stereotypical representation.

Teachers who don't have time to source films for themselves will find a link to a suitable short film here:
http://bit.ly/1nxGlzY

Some typical stereotypes in Hollywood films that you might like to consider are:
- African American:
  athlete, drug dealer, gang member, police officer
- Arab American:
  terrorist, convenience-store clerk
- Asian American:
  doctor, lawyer, CEO
- Hispanic American:
  gang member, factory worker, illegal immigrant
- Irish American:
  drunkard, fire fighter, police officer
- Italian American:
  Mafia boss, gang member, restaurant worker, womaniser
- Jewish American:
  doctor, lawyer, teacher
- Korean American:
  convenience-store clerk, entrepreneur

Action!

☐ Pair the learners and ask them identify as many stereotypes as they can. Set a time limit of three minutes.

☐ Elicit common stereotypes and write them on the board:
-    *Have the learners seen any of these stereotypes in films?*

☐ Tell them they are going to watch a short film clip in which a stereotype is represented:
-    *Can they identify the stereotype and comment on how it is represented?*

☐ Play the film:
-    *Was their reaction to the stereotype positive or negative?*

Post-production

For homework, you can ask the learners to find stereotypical representations in a film clip, and to bring the video to the next class. Show the clips, for the learners to identify and analyse the stereotypes.

Stills for skills

To unlock the learners' writing and speaking skills.

Pre-production

Find a short film which has interaction between two characters. Take separate screenshots of the two main characters in the film.

Teachers who don't have time to source films for themselves will find a link to a suitable short film here: *http://bit.ly/Kh5nYz*

Action!

☐ Show the still image of *one* character from your film on the screen, and ask the learners to discuss the following questions in pairs:
  ◌ *What does he/she look like?*
  ◌ *What kind of person do they think he/she is?*
  ◌ *What is he/she feeling right now?*

☐ When they have finished, get feedback from the whole class.

☐ Now display the image of the *second* character, and repeat the procedure.

☐ Tell the learners that the two characters appear together in the same short film. Ask them to write a short narrative about the two characters:
  ◌ You set a time limit of 10 minutes.
  ◌ You walk round, providing help with language as necessary.

☐ When the learners are ready, ask them to show what they've written to a partner.

☐ Then ask them to read out their narratives to the whole class, and comment on them.

☐ Now show the film, for the learners to compare the story they see in the film with their own narratives.

☐ Hold a plenary discussion:
  ◌ *Were there elements of the learners' stories which were shown in the film?*
  ◌ *How were the learners' narratives similar to the film?*
  ◌ *How were they different?*

Post-production

For homework, the learners can write a composition describing the two characters, their relationship and the story the film tells.

You can find an example of this activity here: *http://bit.ly/1dn5JXy*

Two characters in a still

To unlock the learners' creativity in writing a narrative.

Pre-production

Select a short film which has the two principal characters together in a scene at the beginning.

Take a screenshot of the two characters.

Teachers who don't have time to source films for themselves will find a link to a suitable short film here: *http://bit.ly/1kf51Bl*

Action!

☐ Show the learners the still image with the two characters, and ask them the following questions:
  ◌ *What is the relationship between the two people?*
  ◌ *How are the people feeling right now?*

☐ Tell them that the picture comes from a short film.

☐ Divide the class into groups of three or four, to create a narrative for the film which illustrates the relationship between the two people:
  ◌ You set a time limit of 15 minutes.
  ◌ You walk round, providing help with language as necessary.

☐ The learners read their narrative to a learner from another group.

☐ Get a learner from each group to read out their story to the class. The others comment on the stories.

☐ Show the film.

☐ Ask the learners the following questions:
  ◌ *How did the film make them feel?*
  ◌ *What do they think is going to happen next?*

☐ The learners compare their narratives with that of the film.

Post-production

For homework, you can ask the learners to write a narrative based on the story the film tells, but with an alternative ending.

You can find an example of this activity here: *http://bit.ly/1cMV6NH*

Four-screenshot collage

To be creative, and write an interesting narrative from visual cues.

Pre-production

Select a short film which has a clear narrative structure. Create four screenshots of different parts of the film, and create a collage.

Teachers who don't have time to source films for themselves will find a link to a suitable short film here: *http://bit.ly/191qokx*

Action!

☐ Divide the class into groups of three or four.

☐ Give the learners the collage of screenshots, and tell them that all the images come from a short film.

☐ Their task is to put the images in order and create an interesting narrative:
  - You set a time limit of 15 minutes.
  - You walk round, providing help with language as necessary.

☐ Each learner explains their narrative to a member of a different group.

☐ Invite the learners to read out their narratives to the rest of the class.

☐ Show the short film, for the learners to put the screenshots into the correct order.

☐ Ask the learners to compare their narratives with the story told in the film:
  - *How does the film make them feel?*

Post-production

For homework, the learners can write a more polished version of their narrative.

Alternatively, the learners pick their own film:
  - They select four screenshots and do the same thing they did in class.
  - They show their screenshots to the class.
  - The other learners put the images in order, and create an interesting narrative.

Show the short film, for the learners to compare their narratives with the story told in the film.

You can find an example of this activity here: *http://bit.ly/1lEfdPh*

Six-screenshot story

To write a creative narrative.

Pre-production

Select a short film which has a clear narrative structure. Create six screenshots of different parts of the film.

Teachers who don't have time to source films for themselves will find a link to a suitable short film here: *http://bit.ly/19QCbAx*

Action!

☐ Tell the learners they are going to watch a short film:
  - Give them the title of the film.
  - Show them the six screenshots from the film in chronological order.

☐ Divide the class into groups of three or four.

☐ Ask them to imagine what story the film tells, and to write a narrative based on the title of the film and the six screenshots:
  - You set a time limit of 10 minutes.
  - You walk round, providing help with language as necessary.

☐ Each learner explains their narrative to a member of a different group.

☐ Invite them to read out their narratives to the rest of the class.

☐ Show the film, for the learners to compare their narratives with the story told in the film.

☐ Finally, they discuss the film and talk about how it makes them feel.

Post-production

For homework, you can ask the learners to write a narrative of the film with an alternative ending.

You can find an example of this activity here: *http://bit.ly/1guQUTu*

Up close and emotional

To get the learners to describe strong emotions,
using visual cues.

Pre-production

Find several close-up shots from films which express a range
of emotions.

Enter a search term such as 'close-up shots movies' in
a search engine and select film screenshots, or choose
screenshots from movies which show strong emotions.

Action!

☐ Write the following adjectives on the board:

happy	*frightened*	*angry*	*disappointed*
sad	*surprised*	*tired*	*excited*

☐ Ask the learners to come up with a 'stronger' adjective
for each one, and write these on the board. For example:
sad – miserable

☐ Now ask them to think about situations in which people
feel these emotions.

☐ Write *Close-up shot* on the board:
  ☐ Remind the learners that it is a frame filled with
    just one part of a character or object, often used
    to emphasise the expression on a character's face.

☐ Tell them you are going to show them some close-up shots
from films which show someone expressing a strong
emotion.

☐ Show your close-up shots one by one, inviting the
learners to shout out adjectives and phrases to describe
the emotion.

☐ Pair the learners:
  ☐ One learner acts out an emotion.
  ☐ The other has to identify it.
  ☐ They then exchange roles.

☐ Finally, you can get the learners to take photos of their
partner acting out the emotions on their mobile phones
or other mobile device – and to send you their image files
for the follow-up activity below.

Post-production

You can create a presentation of the images. Show it in the
next lesson, and ask the learners to identify the emotions.

Alternatively, the learners find examples of close-up shots
which appear in their favourite films. They take screenshots
and create a presentation of the images.

Show the presentation in the following lesson, for the
learners to identify the emotions and discuss why the
character was feeling that emotion at that moment.

Poster predictions

To predict the opening scene of a film
from a film poster.

Pre-production

Find a poster of a film your learners are unlikely to know.

You may want to prepare sufficient copies of the poster
for the class. See below.

Action!

☐ Ask the learners:
  ☐ *What kind of information do film posters normally give?*

☐ Try to elicit the following information, and write it on the
board in the form of a chart:
  ☐ Name of the film
  ☐ Names of the actors
  ☐ Slogan or catch-phrase
  ☐ Première date
  ☐ Favourable reviews
  ☐ Award nominations

☐ Put the learners into small groups and show the poster,
or give a copy of the poster to each group.

☐ Tell the learners that their task is to examine:
  ☐ The image(s)
  ☐ The title
  ☐ The story outline
  ☐ The quotes from reviews
  ☐ Any other information

☐ In their groups, the learners have to discuss:
  ☐ *What genre of film is the poster advertising?*
  ☐ *What do they think happens in the first scene in the film?*

☐ After five minutes, elicit predictions from each group.

☐ Now play the opening scene of the film.

☐ Hold a plenary discussion based on these questions:
  ☐ *Which group's predictions were closest to what they saw
    and heard in the opening scene?*
  ☐ *Was there anything in the opening scene that surprised
    them?*

☐ In the same groups, the learners predict the rest of the
film – in 10 minutes.

☐ Elicit the predictions from each group and discuss them.

Post-production

For homework, the learners can watch the rest of the film –
to see if their predictions were correct.

My film – my poster on page 82 is an excellent follow-up
to this activity.

From book to film

To listen to a piece of written text, and compare it with the film version of the same scene.

Pre-production

Find a passage from a novel, short story or graded reader which has been made into a film, and the same extract in a clip from the film version.

Teachers who don't have time to source films for themselves will find a link to a suitable film clip here: *http://bit.ly/1hcCV7K*

Action!

☐ Tell the learners you are going to read an extract from a novel or graded reader:
- As they listen, their task is to visualise the scene in their minds' eye.

☐ Read out the passage.

☐ Pair the learners, to discuss how they visualised the scene:
- *What did the main characters look like?*
- *What was the setting? What were the actions?*

☐ Tell the learners they are going to watch the film version of the scene.

☐ Show the film:
- As they watch, their task is to consider the similarities and differences between their visualisations and the actual film.

☐ Hold a plenary discussion, based on these questions:
- *Did the setting look the way they thought it would?*
- *Did the characters look the way they imagined them?*
- *Was the storyline in the film the same as in the book?*
- *Which did they prefer: the book or the film version?*

Post-production

You can give the learners a passage from a novel, story or reader which has been made into a film. For homework:
- They read the passage and visualise the scene.
- They imagine what it would look like in a film.
- In the next lesson, pairs of learners discuss how they visualised the scene.

Then you show the scene, for them to consider the similarities and differences between their *visualisations* of the scene and what they *see*.

Acknowledgement

This activity is adapted from an activity in *Film* by Susan Stempleski and Barry Tomalin (Oxford University Press).

Sound on – Vision off

To show how moving images present information via combinations of image *and* sound.

Pre-production

Select a short film clip which has interesting dialogue and sounds.

Teachers who don't have time to source films for themselves will find a link to a suitable film clip here: *http://bit.ly/1ixnZPi*

Action!

☐ Tell the learners they are going to *hear*, but not *see*, an extract from a film.

☐ Their task is to guess the visual content:
- *How many people are there?*
- *What do they look like?*
- *What is the action?*
- *When and where is the action taking place?*

☐ Play the film – with *sound only*.

☐ Divide the class into groups of three or four.

☐ The learners work together to infer elements of setting just from the sound components:
- Time and place?
- Indoor/outdoor?
- Action?

☐ Hold a feedback session on the learners' answers.

☐ Now show the film with sound *and* vision.

☐ The learners discuss how accurate their guesses were.

☐ Hold a plenary discussion on how moving images present information via combinations of both sound *and* image.

Post-production

For homework, the learners can choose a scene from one of their favourite films which has an interesting combination of sound and image.

They write a composition in which they describe the way sound and image is used in the scene.

Sketching the sounds

To draw a film scene, and analyse the role
of sound and image.

Pre-production

Select an interesting opening scene of a film.

Action!

☐ Ask the learners to tell you as many types of film as they
can and write the genres on the board. You might like to
include:
  ◦ *Thriller*
  ◦ *Psychological thriller*
  ◦ *Horror film*
  ◦ *Comedy*
  ◦ *Romantic comedy (romcom)*
  ◦ *Science fiction film (Sci-Fi)*
  ◦ *Adventure film*
  ◦ *Fantasy film*
  ◦ *Musical*
  ◦ *Documentary*

☐ Tell the learners they are going to *hear*, but not *see*, the
opening scene of a film:
  ◦ Their task is to say what *type* of film they think it is.

☐ Play the film – with the sound *on* and the vision *off*.

☐ Elicit feedback on the genre of the film.

☐ Tell the learners they are going to hear the opening scene
again:
  ◦ Their task is to draw a sketch of what they expect to see
  on the screen.

☐ Play the film again with sound *on* and vision *off*:
  ◦ Give the learners time to complete their pictures.

☐ In pairs, they compare the drawings and speculate about
what they may see on the screen:
  ◦ Get feedback from the whole class on their expectations.

☐ Show the film – this time with both sound and vision *on*.

☐ The learners compare the sketches they made with what
they see on the screen.

Post-production

For homework, the learners can write a description of the
actual scene they saw in class.

Writing the sounds

To suggest subtitles – for viewers
who are hard of hearing!

Pre-production

Select a short film or clip which has a lot of background
noises.

Teachers who don't have time to source films for themselves
will find a link to a suitable short film here:
http://bit.ly/1nYUpTx

Action!

☐ Tell the learners they are going to watch a short film
in which there are a lot of background noises:
  ◦ Their task is to identify the sounds.

☐ In pairs, they compare their answers.

☐ Tell them to imagine that they work in a post-production
company:
  ◦ Their task is to write the subtitles for 'hard of hearing'
  viewers.

☐ Give them examples, such as:
  ◦ Door opens slowly.
  ◦ Toilet flushes.
  ◦ Wind blows.

☐ Show the film several times:
  ◦ The learners write the subtitles.
  ◦ They then compare their subtitles.

☐ Show the film again.

☐ Pause every time there is a sound, and ask the learners for
their descriptions.

Post-production

The learners can add the subtitles to the film. The subtitles
could be done on YouTube, or with video-editing software
such as Windows Movie Maker or Apple iMovie.

How do they seem?

To imagine a character's appearance and character from listening to them.

Pre-production

Select a clip from a feature-length film, documentary, interview or news item where the main character speaks clearly and distinctively.

Teachers who don't have time to source films for themselves will find a link to a suitable film clip here: *http://bit.ly/1iXZjSW*

Action!

- ☐ Ask the learners what information you can obtain from the way a person speaks.
- ☐ Tell them they are going to *hear*, but not *see*, a character speaking in a film.
- ☐ As they listen, they imagine what the speaker looks like:
  - ☐ *age*
  - ☐ *height*
  - ☐ *build*
  - ☐ *hairstyle*
  - ☐ *face*
  - ☐ *posture*
  - ☐ *clothing*
  - ☐ *accessories*
- ☐ Play the film, with sound only:
  - ☐ The learners have five minutes to write notes on the speaker's *appearance*.
- ☐ Divide the class into pairs, to exchange ideas.
- ☐ Tell them they are going to listen a second time:
  - ☐ As they listen, they speculate on the speaker's character.
- ☐ Play the film again, with sound only:
  - ☐ The learners have five minutes to write notes on the speaker's character.
- ☐ The pairs exchange ideas.
- ☐ Now play the film with the sound *and* image on:
  - ☐ *Is the speaker how they imagined him or her?*
- ☐ Hold a feedback session with the whole class.

Post-production

For homework, the learners can choose one of their favourite film characters. They write about their physical appearance and personality.

How do they sound?

To describe how characters feel, by listening for clues.

Pre-production

Select a short film or clip in which more than one person speaks.

Make a list of adjectives that describe emotion. For example:
- ☐ *angry*
- ☐ *bored*
- ☐ *confused*
- ☐ *envious*
- ☐ *excited*
- ☐ *grateful*
- ☐ *nervous*
- ☐ *relaxed*
- ☐ *relieved*
- ☐ *surprised*
- ☐ *upset*

Teachers who don't have time to source films for themselves will find a link to a suitable short film here: *http://bit.ly/1oVeU6z*

Action!

- ☐ Dictate your list of adjectives to the learners.
- ☐ Tell them they are going to *hear*, but not *see*, a short film:
  - ☐ As they listen, their task is to circle the adjectives which they think best describe the characters' emotions.
- ☐ Play the film – with sound only.
- ☐ Pair the learners, to compare their answers.
- ☐ Play the film with both sound and vision:
  - ☐ *Would they still use the same adjectives to describe the characters?*
- ☐ Hold a feedback session with the whole class.

Post-production

For homework, you can ask the learners to write a description of one of the characters in the film.

It must be ...!

To describe what you hear.

Pre-production

Select a short film which has a number of non-verbal sounds. Write down the sounds, and then add to the list other sounds which are *not* in the film. For example:

- *Someone brushing their teeth*
- *Someone washing their face*
- *Someone having a bath*
- *Someone having a shower*
- *A glass breaking*
- *A radio playing*
- *Someone whistling*

Teachers who don't have time to source films for themselves will find a link to a suitable short film here: *http://bit.ly/Thzd2R*

Action!

- ☐ Dictate your list to the learners.
- ☐ Tell them they are going to *hear*, but not *see*, a short film in which they hear a number of sounds:
  - As they listen, their task is to circle the sounds they hear.
- ☐ Play the film – with sound only.
- ☐ Pair the learners, to compare their answers.
- ☐ Tell them they are now going to *see* the film:
  - As they watch, they check if their answers are correct.
- ☐ Show the film.
- ☐ The learners watch the film again:
  - You pause every time there is a sound.
  - They say what the sound is.

Post-production

For homework, the learners can select short films which have a number of non-verbal sounds:

- They write down the sounds.
- They add to the list other sounds which are *not* in the film.
- In the following lesson, the learners dictate their list or distribute a handout.

You then follow the same procedure as before.

It might be ...!

To listen to a film soundtrack, and speculate about what is on screen.

Pre-production

Select a short film or clip which has clear, discernable actions. Watch the film, and create a list of sentences based on the film which express possibility, probability and certainty. For example:

- *They must be in an airport.*
- *They might be waiting for the same flight.*
- *They might be businessmen.*
- *One man must have just got engaged.*
- *They can't know each other.*

Teachers who don't have time to source films for themselves will find a link to a suitable short film here: *http://bit.ly/1iuxsv1*

Action!

- ☐ Dictate your sentences.
- ☐ Tell the learners they are going to *hear*, but not *see*, a short film:
  - As they listen, they have to decide whether they agree or not with the sentences.
  - If they don't agree with a sentence, they alter it accordingly.
- ☐ Play the film – with sound only.
- ☐ Pair the learners, to speculate on the sentences and justify their answers.
- ☐ Tell them they are now going to see *and* hear the film:
  - As they watch, their task is to decide whether they still agree or not with the sentences.
- ☐ Show the film – with both sound *and* vision.

Post-production

You can play another film with sound only:

- The learners write *their own* sentences to express possibility, probability and certainty.
- They exchange their sentences with a partner, and decide if they agree or not.
- If they don't agree with a sentence, they amend it accordingly.

Show the film with both sound and vision.

Eyewitness account

To compile together a description of a dramatic event.

Pre-production

Find two short film clips which show a dramatic event, such as:

- *A murder*
- *A political assassination*
- *A bank robbery*
- *A fight*
- *An accident*

For teachers who don't have time to source films themselves, here are links to two suitable film clips:
http://bit.ly/1lwECdC
http://bit.ly/1d65uMV

Action!

- ☐ Pair the learners, and divide each pair into 'watchers' and 'listeners':
  - ☐ The watchers will *see* the film.
  - ☐ The listeners will *listen* to the soundtrack, sitting with their back to the screen.
- ☐ Tell the watchers what their task is:
  - ☐ To observe the scene very carefully, and try to remember as much as they can.
- ☐ Tell the listeners what their task is:
  - ☐ To listen to the soundtrack.
  - ☐ To try to imagine what is happening.
  - ☐ To think of questions to ask the watchers about what was shown in the scene.
- ☐ Play the scene.
- ☐ Both learners now face each other and interview each other:
  - ☐ The listeners ask their questions about what happened in the scene.
  - ☐ The watchers give as much information as possible about the events.
- ☐ Play the scene again.
- ☐ The listeners confirm or correct what they understood of the events, as described by the watchers.
- ☐ Finally, play the second dramatic scene:
  - ☐ Reverse the roles.
  - ☐ Repeat the process.

Post-production

For homework, you can ask the learners to write an 'eyewitness statement' for the police, describing exactly what happened in one of the scenes.

Who says what?

To listen for specific expressions, then write and perform dialogues using the same expressions.

Pre-production

Select a film clip or short film which has a lot of interesting expressions. Choose a variety of expressions spoken by characters in the film, and transcribe them.

Action!

- ☐ Dictate your expressions.
- ☐ Put the learners into pairs:
  - ☐ Their task is to compare the expressions they have written down.
- ☐ Elicit or explain the meaning of the expressions as necessary.
- ☐ Tell the learners they are going to watch a film in which they will hear these expressions:
  - ☐ Their task is to say which *character* says which *expression*.
- ☐ Play the film.
- ☐ The learners compare their answers in pairs.
- ☐ Tell them you are going to play the film another time:
  - ☐ This time, their task is to tell you to stop, every time they hear one of the expressions.
- ☐ Play the film again.
- ☐ In pairs, the learners now write their own dialogues using the expressions:
  - ☐ Set a time limit of 10 minutes.
- ☐ The learners roleplay their dialogues.

Post-production

For homework, you can ask the learners to practise their part of the dialogue and memorise their lines.

In the following lesson, they roleplay their dialogues from memory.

On the trail

To listen for specific lines in film trailers.

Pre-production

Find a film trailer website, such as:

- Yahoo Movies – *http://movies.yahoo.com*
- Apple Trailers – *http://apple.com/trailers/*
- Coming Soon – *http://www.comingsoon.net/trailers/*

Choose five trailers you think your learners will enjoy.

Watch each trailer:

- Write two lines of dialogue that *are* in the trailer
- Write two lines of dialogue that are *not* in the trailer.

Prepare a worksheet, with the name of each film and the lines underneath.

Action!

- ☐ Write *Trailer* on the board.

- ☐ Elicit or explain that a trailer is a short advertisement for a feature-length film:
  - *What do you usually see and hear in a trailer?*

- ☐ Elicit or explain that it is very typical to include some of the lines of dialogue from the film.

- ☐ Distribute the worksheet you prepared.

- ☐ Tell the learners that their task is to watch each trailer:
  - They must decide which two lines they *heard*.
  - They must decide which two they *didn't* hear.

- ☐ Play each trailer twice.

- ☐ The learners compare their answers with a partner:
  - *Which trailers did they like the most, and why?*
  - *Which of the films would they like to see?*

Post-production

For homework, the learners could make their own similar activity, based on trailers of films they choose themselves:

- They watch the trailer.
- They write two lines of dialogue that *are* in the trailer and two that *aren't*.

In the following lesson, they play their trailer – for the others to decide which lines they heard, and which they didn't.

Acknowledgement

This activity is adapted from an activity in *Teaching Online* by Nicky Hockley and Lindsay Clandfield (Delta).

Film bingo

To listen for specific words and phrases used in a film clip.

Pre-production

Select a short film or film clip that has quite a lot of dialogue with colloquial expressions:

- Choose five words and expressions used in the film, and write them down.
- Also write down five words and phrases *not* used in the film.

Teachers who don't have time to source films for themselves will find a link to a suitable film clip here: *http://bit.ly/1cp4nXT*

Action!

- ☐ Dictate the 10 words and phrases you have written down.

- ☐ Invite the learners to compare their answers, then elicit the correct words and phrases.

- ☐ Tell the learners that they are going to watch a film clip in which they will hear *some*, but not *all*, of the words and expressions;
  - Their task is to play *Film bingo* and to tick the words they hear.

- ☐ Play the film.

- ☐ The learners compare their answers with a partner.

- ☐ Tell them you are now going to play the film again:
  - Their task is now to call out *Pause!* when they hear one of the words or expressions.

- ☐ Play the film a second time, and pause when the learners tell you to pause.

- ☐ Pair the learners, to write short dialogues using the words and expressions they heard in the clip.

- ☐ They roleplay their dialogues.

Post-production

You can play this game again – using *objects* seen in a clip:

- Write down five objects which appear, and five which don't.
- Dictate the 10 words.

Play the film, for the learners to tick the objects they see.

Voice-over

To put sentences in the correct order,
and decide if they are true or false.

Pre-production

Choose a five-minute clip from a documentary with a voice-over. Write 10 sentences about information in the voice-over script – five should be *true*, and five *false*:

☐ Jumble the words in each sentence so that they are in the wrong order, and make enough copies for the class

(If you think putting the words into order will be too hard for your learners, simply give them the correct sentences.)

For teachers who don't have time to source films themselves, here is a link to a suitable documentary:
http://bit.ly/1dRriO0

Action!

☐ Distribute your handout with the 10 jumbled sentences, or write them on the board and ask the learners to write them down. Tell them:
   ☐ The words in the sentences are not in the correct order.
   ☐ The learners have to put them in the correct order.

☐ When they are ready, they compare with a partner.

☐ Elicit the correct answers, and write them on the board.

☐ Write *Voice-over* on the board:
   ☐ Elicit or explain that a voice-over is words spoken in a film, television programme or ad by a person who is not seen.

☐ Tell the learners that the sentences refer to the voice-over of a short clip from a documentary which they are going to watch:
   ☐ *Are the sentences true or false, according to the information in the film?*

☐ Show the film:
   ☐ The learners compare their answers.

☐ Show the film a second time:
   ☐ The learners tell you to pause the film when you come to the parts which give information as to whether the sentences are true or false.

Post-production

For homework, the learners can choose a five-minute clip from a documentary, and write five *true/false* sentences.

In the following lesson, each learner writes their sentences on the board, the others watch and listen carefully to the film and decide whether they are true or false.

You can find an example of this activity here:
http://bit.ly/U3ANq5

The sound of music

To describe emotions generated by film music.

Pre-production

Find a short film or clip which has emotive music, but no dialogue.

Teachers who don't have time to source films for themselves will find a link to a suitable short film here:
http://bit.ly/KiDLS7

Action!

☐ Tell the learners you are going to play a short piece of music:
   ☐ You want them to close their eyes and to think of any emotions that come to mind as they listen.

☐ Play the film – with sound *only*.

☐ Pair the learners, to share the emotions they felt.

☐ Tell them that the music is used in a short film or clip:
   ☐ *What images do they imagine accompany the music?*

☐ Play the film with the sound *and* image on.

☐ Hold a plenary discussion:
   ☐ *Was the film how they imagined?*
   ☐ *Does the music suit the film?*
   ☐ *How did the film make them feel?*

☐ Ask the learners what they think is going to happen *after* the scene you played.

Post-production

For homework, the learners can write a narrative about what happened *before* or what happens *after* the scene.

This activity can be used with any film clip which has emotive music and no dialogue.

You can see any example of this activity here:
http://bit.ly/1cqKnEf

Music, music, music

*To revise film genres, and discuss the music
used in the different genres.*

Pre-production

Find a film which has atmospheric music over the opening titles which is typical of a particular genre. It is best *not* to choose a very well-known film with opening credits music that the learners will instantly recognise.

Hundreds of beautiful opening credits can be found here: Art of the Title – *http://www.artofthetitle.com/*

Teachers who don't have time to source films for themselves will find a link to a suitable film clip here: *http://bit.ly/1gjHuKq*

Action!

☐ Write *Film genres* on the board, and ask the learners to name as many genres as they can:
   ☐ You can revise important film genres, such the ones opposite.

☐ Elicit examples of each genre.

☐ Write *Opening titles*, and elicit or explain that the opening credits are the captions which appear at the beginning of a film:
   ☐ You can revise the information they normally give – see opposite.

☐ Ask the learners to think about what kind of *music* accompanies the opening titles in some of the genres they mentioned earlier.

☐ Elicit adjectives that describe the music.

☐ Tell the learners they are going to hear the music from a film.

☐ Pair them, and tell them to predict:
   The genre   The title   The era

☐ Play the film, with *sound* only.

☐ Elicit the predictions, and write them on the board.

☐ Now play the film with sound *and* vision – until the end of the titles.

☐ The learners compare their predictions with what they see and hear.

Post-production

Give the learners the link to Art of the Title: *http://www.artofthetitle.com/*

For homework, they can watch opening titles from a variety of film genres. For each film, they write down adjectives to describe the type of music used.

Film genres

☐ Comedy

☐ Romantic comedy (romcom)

☐ Romance

☐ Thriller

☐ Psychological thriller

☐ Horror

☐ Science fiction (Sci-Fi)

☐ Drama

☐ Historical drama

☐ Costume drama

☐ Adventure

☐ Fantasy

☐ Western

Opening titles

☐ Title of the film

☐ Cast

☐ Director

☐ People involved in making the film:
   ☐ Film studio
   ☐ Producer
   ☐ Executive producer
   ☐ Director of photography
   ☐ Editor
   ☐ Costume designer
   ☐ Screenwriter

On the right track

To predict the story a film tells, by listening to music from the soundtrack.

Pre-production
Select a film which you think your learners will be unfamiliar with, and select an interesting scene and also some songs from the soundtrack.

Action!

☐ Tell the learners they are going to listen to a musical selection from a film:
  ◦ As they listen, they should visualise the images that come to mind.

☐ Play the music you selected.

☐ Pair the learners:
  ◦ *What images did they visualise?*

☐ Divide the class into groups of three or four.

☐ Tell the learners that the music comes from the soundtrack of a film.

☐ Their task is to predict the story the film tells:
  ◦ You set a time limit of 10 minutes.
  ◦ You walk round, providing help with language as necessary.

☐ Hold a feedback session on the learners' predictions.

☐ Now show two or three scenes from the film, and ask the learners to see how accurate their predictions were.

☐ Discuss.

Post-production
For homework, you can give the learners a link to a song from a film scene they are unlikely to know:
  ◦ They listen to the song.
  ◦ They imagine what they would see in that scene.
  ◦ They write a description of the scene.

In the next lesson, the learners compare their descriptions. Show the film and ask them to compare their descriptions with what they actually see.

See, hear, feel ...

To respond to the instrumental music used in a film.

Pre-production
Find a short film which has instrumental music, but no dialogue.

Teachers who don't have time to source films for themselves will find a link to a suitable short film here: *http://bit.ly/KiDLS7*

Action!

☐ Play the film, with sound only.

☐ Ask the learners to listen to the music.

☐ Invite them to write about what they *saw* (in their mind's eye) while listening to the music:
  ◦ Set a time limit of five minutes.

☐ Play the music a second time.

☐ Invite the learners to write about what they *heard* while listening to the music.
  ◦ Set a time limit of five minutes.

☐ Play the music a third time.

☐ Invite the learners to write about what they *felt* while listening to the music:
  ◦ They compare everything they wrote in pairs.

☐ Hold a plenary discussion on what the learners *saw, heard* and *felt*.

☐ Finally, play the film clip with both sound and image *on*.
  ◦ *Are the emotions they feel different?*

Post-production
For homework, the learners can choose a piece of instrumental music from a film they enjoy. They should listen to the music several times and write about what they *saw, what they heard* and *what they felt*.

Acknowledgement
This activity is adapted from an activity in *Being Creative* by Chaz Pugliese (Delta).

Character study

To describe a character in a film, and make notes
to justify the description.

Pre-production

Prepare a circle with an inner circle, which you will be using
for a film which your learners have watched.

Action!

☐ After the learners have watched a film or film clip,
draw on the board a circle with an inner circle, and ask
the learners to copy it in their notebooks.

☐ Assign a film character to each learner.

☐ Tell the learners that their task is to do the following:
- Write words in the *inner* circle which describe
the true personality of the character.
- Make notes that support their descriptions – for
example, the character's words or actions.
- Write words in the *outer* circle which describe
what other characters think of the character.
- Make notes that support their descriptions – for
example, the words and actions of other characters.

☐ The learners complete their circles and notes individually:
- You set a time limit of 10 minutes.
- You walk round, providing help with language as
necessary.

☐ When the learners are ready, divide the class into groups
of three or four, making sure that each member of the
group has a different character.

☐ Ask the learners to take turns describing the 'true
characters' and what others think of the character.
The other group members listen:
- *Do they agree with the description, or not?*
- *Can they provide any other words to describe
the character?*

☐ Hold a plenary discussion, based on the descriptions
of the characters.

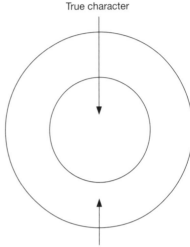

True character

What other characters think of him or her

Post-production

The learners can write a composition, comparing what
other characters think of the character and what they are
really like.

Alternatively, they choose their favourite film character
and repeat the procedure they did in class:
- They draw a circle with an inner circle.
- They write the true personality of the character in
the inner circle, and what others think of him or her
in the outer circle.

Based on the words they have used in the circles, they write
a composition comparing what other characters think of the
character and what he or she is really like.

Character webs

To describe a character and write a composition.

Pre-production

Prepare a character web, and four adjectives that describe a character in a film which your learners have recently watched. Our example: *Braveheart*.

Action!

- ☐ After watching the film, draw your character web on the board, and write in it your four adjectives:
  - ▫ *Do the learners think these are good adjectives to describe the character?*
  - ▫ *Can they think of any other adjectives to describe the character?*

- ☐ Draw an *empty* character web on the board, and ask the learners to copy it into their notebooks.

- ☐ Tell them they are going to describe one of the characters they have seen in the film.

- ☐ Assign a character to each learner.

- ☐ Their task is to do the following:
  - ▫ Write the name of the character in the centre circle.
  - ▫ Label each of the four outer circles with an adjective that describes the character.
  - ▫ Make notes that justify the descriptions – for example, the character's words or actions, or the words and actions of other characters.

- ☐ The learners complete their character webs and notes individually:
  - ▫ You set a time limit of five minutes.
  - ▫ You walk round, providing help with language as necessary.

- ☐ When the learners are ready, divide the class into groups of three or four, making sure that each member of the group has a different character.

- ☐ They take turns describing their characters. The other group members listen:
  - ▫ *Do they agree with the description, or not?*
  - ▫ *Can they provide any other words to describe the character?*

- ☐ Hold a plenary discussion, based on the descriptions of the characters.

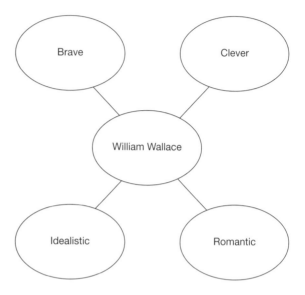

Post-production

The learners can use the information in their character webs to write a composition describing the character.

Alternatively, they can create webs for a character who appears in one of their favourite films.

In the next class, they explain their character web to a partner and justify their description by referring to the character's words and actions, or to the words and actions of other characters.

Acknowledgement

This activity is adapted from an activity in *Film* by Susan Stempleski and Barry Tomalin (Oxford University Press).

Character comparisons

To compare two film characters.

Pre-production

Prepare a Venn diagram, with words that describe two characters in a film which your learners have recently watched. Our example: *Casablanca*.

Action!

☐ After watching the film or film clip, draw your Venn diagram on the board, and write in it the words to describe the two characters:
- *Do the learners think these are good words to describe the characters?*
- *Can they think of any other words to describe the characters?*

☐ Draw a new *blank* Venn diagram on the board:
- In the circle on the left, write the name of one character.
- In the circle on the right, write the name of the other character.
- In the space where the circles overlap, write *Both*.

☐ Ask the learners to copy it into their notebooks.

☐ Tell them they are going to use the Venn diagram, to compare two of the main characters they have seen in the film.

☐ Their task is to write the following:
- Words to describe the first character in the circle on the left.
- Words to describe the second character in the circle on the right.
- Anything they have in common in the space where the circles overlap.

☐ Ask the learners to complete their diagrams:
- You set a time limit of five minutes.
- You walk round, providing help with language as necessary.

☐ When they are ready, pair them to compare the words they have used to describe the two characters.

☐ They write five sentences comparing the two characters, using the adjectives they have used in their diagrams.

☐ When they are ready, ask them to compare their sentences with their partner.

☐ Hold a plenary discussion, comparing the two characters.

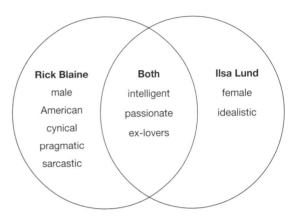

Post-production

For homework, the learners can use the information in their completed diagram to write a composition in which they compare the two characters.

Alternatively, they choose two characters from one of their favourite films:
- They create a Venn diagram.
- They complete it with adjectives to describe the characters.

They then write a composition in which they compare the two characters.

Acknowledgement

This activity is adapted from an activity in *Film* by Susan Stempleski and Barry Tomalin (Oxford University Press).

First impressions

To predict what a character will do next in a film.

Pre-production

Select a film in which one of the main characters appears in the first scene and changes physically and emotionally during the film:

☐ Find the opening scene.

☐ Find a scene from later in the film in which the character has changed a lot.

For teachers who don't have time to source films themselves, here are links to suitable film clips:
http://bit.ly/1nQ1Aka
http://bit.ly/1nQ1Aka

Action!

☐ Show the first scene, and pause when the character first appears.

☐ Pair the learners, and ask them to describe what the character looks like and what clothes they are wearing.

☐ When the learners have finished, elicit the vocabulary that describes the appearance of the character:
  ▫ *What type of person do they think the character is?*
  ▫ *What do they expect him or her to do in the film?*

☐ Hold a plenary discussion, based on their expectations.

☐ Tell the learners they are going to watch a clip from later in the film, in which the character has changed:
  ▫ *How has the character changed?*
  ▫ *Do their opinions of him or her change?*

☐ To help them analyse the character, you might like to point out that characters we meet in a film are revealed to us in a number of ways:
  ▫ What they look like.
  ▫ How they behave in different situations.
  ▫ How they interact with others.
  ▫ How they speak or sound.
  ▫ The music associated with them.

☐ Show the film:
  ▫ You could pause and discuss the character's feelings at emotional moments.

☐ Hold a plenary session, based on how the character has changed.

Post-production

For homework, the learners can choose one of their favourite films in which a character changes. They write a composition describing the changes.

Lasting impressions

To empathise with a character and predict what will happen to him or her in the next 10 years.

Pre-production

Select a short film or clip which has distinct and clearly defined characters.

Teachers who don't have time to source films for themselves will find a link to a suitable short film here:
http://bit.ly/1oVeU6z

Action!

☐ Tell the learners they are going to watch a short film or clip in which they will see several characters:
  ▫ As they watch, their task is to consider the personality of each character.

☐ Show the film.

☐ Assign each learner a character.

☐ Ask them to imagine that *they* are the character:
  ▫ Their task is to decide what will happen to them in the next 10 years.

☐ Each learner writes a paragraph in the first person, describing the next 10 years of their character:
  ▫ You set a time limit of 15 minutes.
  ▫ You walk round, providing help with language as necessary.

☐ Pair the learners:
  ▫ They explain to each other their character's future in the first person.
  ▫ Their partner asks questions.

☐ Hold a feedback session on the future of each character.

Post-production

For homework, you can ask the learners to write a letter from the perspective of their character to another character in the film.

You can find an example of this activity here:
http://bit.ly/1oHpErt

Between the lines

To see how paralinguistic factors are an important part
of understanding a film.

Pre-production

Find a scene in which the characters have strong feelings
which they express in body language or facial expressions,
rather than in words.

Action!

☐ Write *Read between the lines* on the board:
  ▫ Either elicit or explain that it means to try to
    understand what is meant by something which is
    not written or said explicitly or openly.

☐ Write *Body language* on the board:
  ▫ Either elicit examples or pre-teach verbs connected
    with body language – such as the ones opposite.

☐ Write *Facial expressions* on the board:
  ▫ Either elicit examples or pre-teach verbs connected
    with facial expressions – such as the ones opposite.

☐ Tell the learners that they are going to watch a scene
  in which the characters:
  ▫ have strong feelings about what is happening and
    what others are saying;
  ▫ do not express these feelings in words.

☐ Show the film.

☐ The learners watch the scene:
  ▫ Their task is to read between the lines, to find the
    characters' true feelings – by focusing on their body
    language and facial expressions.

☐ Pair the learners;
  ▫ Their task is to discuss the characters' real feelings
    and describe the body language and facial expressions
    which the characters use to show them.

☐ Show the film a second time.

☐ Ask the learners to tell you to pause when a character uses
  body language or facial expressions that show their true
  feelings:
  ▫ *What is the character feeling?*
  ▫ *How does he/she express these feelings?*

Post-production

The learners can imagine they are a character in the film
who doesn't express their feelings through words.

They write a letter to another character in the scene,
describing their real emotions and why they couldn't
show them.

Body language	Facial expressions
fidget	*smile*
stand up straight	*grin*
slouch	*frown*
lean closer	*scowl*
lean away	*pout*
fold your arms	*wink*
drum your fingers	*raise your eyebrows*
nod your head	*roll your eyes*
shake your head	*grimace*
stroke your chin	*wince*
	blush

Show some emotion!

To identify and describe emotions shown
by characters in a film clip.

Pre-production

Find a film clip which shows a display of strong emotions,
either positive or negative, or a combination.

Teachers who don't have time to source films for themselves
will find a link to a suitable film clip here:
http://bit.ly/KiQ80z

Action!

☐ Depending on the level of the class, either elicit or pre-
teach vocabulary for describing and expressing emotions.
For example:

cold	*screaming*
cool	*crying*
calm	*crying with joy*
nervous	*laughing hysterically*
excited	*delighted*
anxious	*ecstatic*
stressed	*enchanted*
insulted	*adoring*
shouting	

☐ Tell the learners they are going to watch a film clip
in which strong emotions are displayed:
   □ Their task is to identify them.

☐ Play the film once, and ask the learners to identify
any emotions they see.

☐ Play the film again. This time:
   □ Pause at key moments.
   □ Ask the learners to describe the emotions shown
by the characters.

☐ Hold a plenary discussion based on these questions:
   □ *Why do the characters feel these emotions?*
   □ *Were the learners convinced by the actors' portrayals
of these emotions?*

Post-production

For homework, the learners can find a film clip they like,
in which the characters show strong emotions:
□ They watch the film.
□ They write down the emotions shown by the characters
and a brief explanation for these emotions.

In the next lesson, the learners show their clips, and ask the
others what emotions they see. The learner can then give
their explanation for these emotions.

Famous film lines

To start speaking about scripts,
in an activity involving favourite quotes.

Pre-production

Find a film which has a compilation of the top ten film lines,
or find a number of films with lines from different films.

For teachers who don't have time to source films themselves,
here are links to two suitable film quote compilation films:
http://bit.ly/1cpe7RK
http://bit.ly/1cpe7RK

Action!

☐ Tell the learners one of *your* favourite film lines:
   □ You say why you like it so much.

☐ Ask them to tell a partner *their* favourite film line:
   □ They say why they like it so much.

☐ Show a film of the 'top ten' film lines.

☐ The first time the learners watch it, they should try to
identify the *films*.

☐ Elicit the films.

☐ Tell the learners they are going to watch the film again:
   □ Their task is now to write down the exact *words*
in each line.

☐ Play the film as many times as necessary.

☐ Elicit the correct *lines*.

☐ Pair the learners, to discuss each line and talk about
which ones they like the best.

☐ Finally, ask them to translate some of their favourite
famous lines from films in *their* language into English.

Post-production

For homework, you can ask the learners to find five other
film lines that they like:
□ Their task is to create a quiz worksheet with incomplete
versions of the lines.
□ For example, from *Gone With The Wind*:
□ *Frankly, my dear …* (I don't give a damn!)

In the following lesson, they give the worksheet to a partner,
who has to try to complete the film lines.

Scrutinising a script

To analyse part of a film script, and to note down scriptwriting conventions.

Pre-production

Go to a script site such as Daily Script (*www.dailyscript.com*) and find a film which you think your students would like. Download the script, and find a scene of no longer than one page which has interesting dialogue and action:

- Make copies of the script of that scene.
- Find and cue the scene on a DVD.
- Make sure you are familiar with scriptwriting conventions, such as those opposite.
- Make sufficient copies of the conventions.

Teachers who don't have time to source films for themselves will find a link to a suitable film clip here: *http://bit.ly/1hczldP*

Action!

- Write *Scriptwriter* on the board for your learners, and elicit or explain that a scriptwriter is the person who writes the written form of a film, TV show, etc:
  - *What do they know about the 'conventions' of scriptwriting?*
  - *In other words, how might a film script be different from a passage in a novel?*
- Divide the class into groups of three or four.
- Tell the learners that you are going to give them part of a film script:
  - Their task is to write down any scriptwriting conventions they notice.
- Give them the film script, and provide an example of a scriptwriting convention, such as:
  A description of the setting is given at the beginning of each new scene.
- The learners read the script, find scriptwriting conventions and take notes:
  - Set a time limit of 15 minutes.
- Ask the class what conventions they noticed:
  - You write a list on the board.
  - Then you give them the handout with the conventions.
- Point out any screenwriting conventions that the learners have not noticed.
- Ask the learners to visualise the scene they read earlier.
- Now show the scene:
  - *Is it similar to what they visualised?*
  - *Does having read the script help them understand the scene better?*

Scriptwriting conventions

- A description of the setting is given at the beginning of each new scene.
- Each scene is numbered.
- Abbreviations are used in describing the setting. For example: INT for *interior* and EXT for *exterior*.
- Capital letters are used for setting locations and times. For example: EXT ROOF TERRACE – DAY
- Capital letters are used for camera shots and movements. For example: CLOSE SHOT and LONG SHOT
- Dialogue is centred on the page.
- Dialogue is in lower case.
- There are no quotation marks around lines of dialogue.
- Stage directions are:
  - in brackets. For example: (He pulls out a piece of paper.)
  - in the present tense.
  - on separate lines from the dialogue.
- The names of characters are:
  - in capital letters: For example: SCOTTIE
  - in the centre of the page.
  - on separate lines from the text.

Post-production

You can give the learners the address of a script site such as Daily Script (*www.dailyscript.com*) and ask them to find a film they like, download the script and find and read some of their favourite scenes.

Acknowledgement

This activity is adapted from an activity in *Film* by Susan Stempleski and Barry Tomalin (Oxford University Press).

Discussing a dialogue I

To read, analyse and perform a dialogue.

Pre-production

Select a short film or scene which has clear and distinct dialogue between two characters. Transcribe the dialogue and make sufficient copies for the class.

Action!

☐ Distribute the transcription.

☐ Tell the learners to read it, and ask them to consider the following questions:
  - *Who is talking?*
  - *What are they talking about?*
  - *Where are they?*

☐ Pair the learners, to read the dialogue.

☐ Invite volunteers to act out the dialogue in front of the whole class.

☐ Play the film.

☐ Hold a plenary discussion based on the following questions:
  - *What differences are there between their performance of the dialogue and the original?*
  - *Did anything surprise them about the characters, the atmosphere or the context?*

☐ The learners act out the dialogue again – in light of their answers in the previous stage.

☐ Finally, invite them to come to the front of the class and perform their dialogues, while standing next to the screen with the vision *on* but the sound *off*.

Post-production

Dialogue dubbing (on page 85) and *Filming a dialogue* (on page 92) are excellent for following up this activity.

Discussing a dialogue II

To listen to, analyse and perform a dialogue.

Pre-production

Select a short film or scene which has interesting dialogue between two characters. Transcribe the dialogue.

Action!

☐ Tell the learners they are going to watch a short film or scene in which they hear two characters having a conversation:
  - Their task is to identify the topic of the conversation.

☐ Play the film.

☐ Elicit the topic of the conversation.

☐ Distribute the transcript, or write it on the board and ask the learners to copy it.

☐ The learners read the transcript – you help, as needed.

☐ Tell them they are going to watch the film again:
  - Their task is to underline the words in the dialogue which are *stressed*.

☐ Play the film again.

☐ Pair the learners, to discuss the words they underlined.

☐ Go through the dialogue with the whole class:
  - Their task is to come to a consensus on which words are stressed.

☐ The learners practise their dialogues in pairs.

☐ Invite them to come to the front of the class and perform their dialogues, standing next to the screen with the vision *on* but the sound *off*.

☐ Now play the film with both sound and vision *on*.

☐ The learners compare *their* performances with the original.

Post-production

For homework, the learners can choose a short scene from one of their favourite films which has interesting dialogue between two characters:
  - They transcribe the dialogue, or find it on a script website such as Daily Script (*www.dailyscript.com*).
  - They watch the film, and underline the words which are stressed in the dialogue.

In the next lesson, they practise the dialogue with a partner.

Dialogue deduction

To use visual and stylistic clues to reconstruct
a dialogue, and act it out.

Pre-production
Select a film scene or short film which has an interesting
dialogue between two characters.

Action!

☐ Tell the learners they are going to see, but not hear,
an extract from a film. Their task is to observe and try
to remember:
- *How many people are there?*
- *What do they look like?*
- *What is the action?*
- *When and where is the action taking place?*

☐ Show the film with the vision *on*.

☐ Pair the learners, to tell their partner what they can
remember about the scene.

☐ Divide the class into groups of three or four, and tell them
what their task is:
- To reconstruct the dialogue in the scene.
- To imagine what the characters are saying.

☐ Set a time limit of 10 minutes. Walk round, providing
help with language as necessary.

☐ The learners practise their dialogues in pairs.

☐ Invite them to come to the front of the class and perform
their dialogues, while standing next to the screen with the
vision *on* – but the sound *off*.

☐ Now play the film with both sound and vision *on*.

☐ The learners compare *their* dialogues with the original.

Post-production
For homework, the learners can practise their part of the
dialogue until they have memorised it.

In the following lesson, they perform their dialogues
from memory in pairs.

Dialogue dictogloss

To reconstruct a dialogue together, and act it out.

Pre-production
Select a short film which has dialogue between two
characters.

Action!

☐ Tell the learners they are going to watch a short film
in which they will hear a conversation between two
characters.

☐ Divide the class into two groups:
- One group will concentrate on what Character 1
is saying, and ignore Character 2.
- One group will concentrate on what Character 2
is saying, and ignore Character 1.

☐ Each group will write down key words and expressions
that their character says:
- Point out that it is not necessary to write down
everything their character says – just key words and
short phrases.

☐ Show the film twice.

☐ The learners compare the notes they made with other
members of their group.

☐ Pair each learner with a member of the other group:
- They re-write the whole script.
- They use their imagination to complete any part
of the script they think is missing.

☐ Set a time limit of 10 minutes.

☐ The learners now roleplay their script:
- One learner is Character 1.
- One learner is Character 2.

☐ Invite volunteers to come to the front of the class and
act out their dialogues – while you play the film with
no sound.

☐ The learners watch the film again, and compare *their*
scripts with the original.

Post-production
You can give the learners the transcript. For homework:
- They practise the dialogue.
- They try to remember the lines of their character.

In the following lesson, they roleplay the dialogue
from memory.

Scrambled scripts

To put jumbled expressions from a dialogue
in the correct order.

Pre-production

Select a short film or scene which has a number of
interesting expressions:

- Prepare six expressions from the scene.
- Jumble them up, ensuring they are not in chronological
  order.

Teachers who don't have time to source films for themselves
will find a link to a suitable film clip here:
http://bit.ly/1ar456Q

Action!

- ☐ Dictate your six expressions.
- ☐ Tell the learners they are going to watch a short film or
  scene in which they will hear the six expressions:
  - Their task is to put them into chronological order.
- ☐ Show the scene twice.
- ☐ Pair the learners, and give them five minutes to sequence
  the expressions correctly.
- ☐ Show the scene again, and check the sequencing.
- ☐ The learners decide:
  - *Who said the expressions?*
  - *To whom?*
  - *What about?*
  - *Why?*
  - *In what manner?*
- ☐ Show the scene again, pause at each expression and check
  the answers.

Post-production

For homework, the learners can choose a scene from one of
their favourite films which has a lot of dialogue:

- They watch the scene and write down six expressions.
- They jumble them up.

In the next lesson, each learner dictates their expressions to
the rest of the learners. They show the film, for the others
to put the expressions in order.

Acknowledgement

This activity is adapted from an activity in *Using Authentic
Film in the Language Classroom* by Jane Sherman
(Cambridge University Press).

Text transformation

To recognise register, and practise shifts of register
in a film script.

Pre-production

Select a film clip with very either formal or informal register,
and prepare a transcription of the scene for the learners.

Teachers who don't have time to source films for themselves
will find a link to a suitable film clip here:
http://bit.ly/1dki40F

Action!

- ☐ Brainstorm formal and informal expressions.
- ☐ Tell the learners they are going to watch a short film clip:
  - Their task is to say whether it is formal or informal.
- ☐ Show the film.
- ☐ Ask the learners:
  - *Is it formal or informal?*
  - *Which words or expressions helped them decide?*
- ☐ Pair the learners, and give them a transcript of the scene.
- ☐ Their task is to transform the dialogue into a different
  register:
  - If it is a formal dialogue, they should transform it into
    an informal register.
  - If it is informal, they should transform it into a formal
    register.
- ☐ Set a time limit of 10 minutes and walk round, providing
  help with language as necessary.
- ☐ The learners practise their new dialogues in pairs.
- ☐ Invite pairs to lip-synch their dialogues in front of the class.

Post-production

For homework, the learners can choose a scene from one of
their favourite films which has very formal language or very
informal language:

- They transcribe the dialogue.
- Alternatively, they go to a script site such as Daily Script
  (*www.dailyscript.com*) and copy it.

They transform the dialogue into a formal or informal
register.

Acknowledgement

This activity is adapted from an activity in *Using Authentic
Film in the Language Classroom* by Jane Sherman
(Cambridge University Press).

Speech strategies

To listen to a speech, recognise the rhetorical techniques and practise reading it aloud.

Pre-production

Rhetoric is the art or skill of speaking or writing formally and effectively, especially as a way to persuade or influence people. Select a scene with a dramatic speech which uses rhetorical techniques.

Hundreds of excellent speeches and transcriptions from American films can be found at American Rhetoric: *http://bit.ly/1dxx8Us*

Teachers who don't have time to source films for themselves will find a link to a suitable film clip here: *http://bit.ly/1aedjzT*

Action!

☐ Ask the learners if they can think of any dramatic speeches they have seen in films.

☐ Elicit or explain the techniques which can make a good speech, such as:
  - ☐ *Repetition*
  - ☐ *Heavy word stress*
  - ☐ *Exaggeration*
  - ☐ *Pausing for effect*
  - ☐ *Anger*
  - ☐ *Sorrow*
  - ☐ *Gratitude*
  - ☐ *Anecdotes*

☐ Add *Rhetorical questions* (a question asked not to elicit a specific answer, but rather to encourage the listener to consider a message or viewpoint).

☐ Tell the learners they are going to watch a speech from a film:
  - ☐ Their task is to notice the rhetorical techniques used by the speaker.

☐ Show the film.

☐ Divide the class into groups of three or four:
  - ☐ Their task is to identify and describe the techniques used.

☐ Show the film a second time.

☐ Hold a feedback session on the rhetorical techniques used.

☐ Give the learners the transcription of the speech:
  - ☐ They listen to the speech.
  - ☐ They underline the words which are stressed heavily.

☐ Play the film with sound only.

☐ Pair the learners, to take turns reading the speech aloud with appropriate stress and intonation.

Post-production

For homework, the learners can read the speech aloud several times, then record it, or part of it, on their PC, laptop or mobile device:
- ☐ They send you the sound file.
- ☐ You watch the film and give them individual feedback on their presentation and pronunciation.

In the following lesson, hold a group feedback session on their presentations.

Alternatively, the learners choose a speech from a film which they like, and find a transcription of it at a script site such as Daily Script (*www.dailyscript.com*):
- ☐ They read it aloud several times.
- ☐ They record the speech on a webcam or mobile device.
- ☐ They send you the sound file.
- ☐ You watch the film and give them individual feedback on their presentation and pronunciation.

In the following lesson, hold a group feedback session.

Acknowledgement

This activity is adapted from an activity in *Using Authentic Film in the Language Classroom* by Jane Sherman (Cambridge University Press).

Viral videos

To discuss why films become viral,
and analyse a viral film.

Pre-production

Find a viral film (a short film that becomes popular through the process of internet sharing, typically through film-sharing websites, social media and email) which you think your learners will enjoy.

For teachers who don't have time to source films themselves, here is a link to a suitable viral film:
http://bit.ly/1bz43FU

Action!

☐ Ask the learners to think of examples of viral films which they have seen. Explain what a viral film is, if necessary:
    ☐ *Why are these films so popular?*

☐ Tell them they are going to watch a viral film:
    ☐ Their task is to analyse the film and explain why they think it is so popular.

☐ Show the film.

☐ Put the learners into groups of three, to discuss why the film is so popular.

☐ Finally, hold a plenary discussion based on these questions:
    ☐ *Why do they think the film is so popular?*
    ☐ *Who does the film appeal to?*
    ☐ *Would they share the film?*

Post-production

For homework, you can ask the learners to choose a viral film they like and then write a review, based on the following questions:
    ☐ *Why do they like it in particular?*
    ☐ *Why is the film so popular in general?*
    ☐ *Who does the film appeal to?*

You can also select a viral film on YouTube which has caused a lot of controversy. (See *http://bit.ly/1l0YhBx.*)

You go to the 'Comments' section of the video and choose three very *favourable* comments and three very *unfavourable*.

Copy them into a Word document, jumble them and prepare copies for the learners:
    ☐ *Do they ever read the YouTube comments section?*
    ☐ *If so, what sorts of comments do people make?*

Give them the jumbled worksheet:
    ☐ They underline the words and expressions which helped them decide which are favourable/unfavourable.

The learners write a commentary in a short paragraph. You correct any mistakes, before they add it to YouTube.

Branded shorts

To watch a short film, and describe what the creators
are trying to communicate.

Pre-production

Select a 'branded short' (a short film which has been created for a company or product).

Teachers who don't have time to source films for themselves will find a link to a suitable short film here:
http://bit.ly/1hldOzK

Action!

☐ Tell the learners they are going to watch a short film which is actually an advertisement for a company or product – a 'branded short':
    ☐ Their task is to decide what type of company or product is being advertised.

☐ Show the film:
    ☐ So the learners don't see the company's name or logo, you may have to pause before the closing credits.

☐ Divide the class into groups of three or four:
    ☐ The learners discuss what type of company or product they think has commissioned the film or is being advertised.
    ☐ They give reasons to support their opinion.

☐ Hold a feedback session on their opinions.

☐ Show the film a second time:
    ☐ Pause when the advertiser's name or logo appears in the closing credits.
    ☐ Ask the learners what they know about the company or product.

☐ Hold a plenary session based on these questions:
    ☐ *How does the film support the brand?*
    ☐ *What is the film saying about the company or product?*
    ☐ *Why is advertising increasingly using short films?*

Post-production

For homework, the learners can find a branded short they like.

They write a review, answering the following questions:
    ☐ *How does the film support the brand?*
    ☐ *What is the film saying to the audience about the company or product?*

You can see an example of this activity here:
http://bit.ly/KnY2pf

Response films

To respond to popular viral films and videos
which have been commissioned by companies.

Pre-production

Select a short film commissioned by a large company, which has gone viral and provoked a response video.

For teachers who don't have time to source films themselves, here are links to two suitable short films:
http://bit.ly/1m73wF   *http://bit.ly/1p07ywu*
and two films which parody the original films:
http://bit.ly/1iasSOX   *http://bit.ly/1fAOsYf*

Action!

☐ Introduce the theme of the short film the learners are going to watch:
- ☐ Pre-teach any necessary vocabulary.
- ☐ Dictate some discussion questions.
- ☐ Ask the learners to discuss them in pairs.

☐ Tell the learners they are going to watch a short film on the theme which they were discussing.

☐ Show the film.

☐ Divide the class into small groups:
- ☐ *How did the film make them feel?*
- ☐ *What was their opinion of it?*

☐ Tell the learners that the film was commissioned by a company. Give the name of the company:
- ☐ *Do they know anything about it?*
If they don't, give them some information about it:
- ☐ *Do they still feel the same about the film, knowing that it was commissioned by a big company?*

☐ Tell them that a film-maker has made a new film which criticises or parodies the original film in some way – a 'response' film:
- ☐ *How do they think the film-maker may have criticised or parodied the film?*

☐ Show the film.

☐ Get feedback from the learners:
- ☐ *How does the film criticise or parody the original?*

Post-production

For homework, the learners can find their own response video to a viral video. They watch both the viral video and the response video, and then write a short composition in which they explain how the response video criticises or parodies the viral video.

You can see examples of this activity here:
http://bit.ly/1lEKFyi
http://bit.ly/1d9MD4x

One-second films

To describe what is happening in a film,
and talk about interesting moments from it.

Pre-production

Select a film which is a compilation of one-second-long films.

For teachers who don't have time to source films themselves, here is a link to a suitable compilation film:
http://bit.ly/1a5FMuO

Action!

☐ Ask the learners what can happen in a second. Brainstorm ideas with the whole class.

☐ Tell them they are going to watch a short film in which there are 60 clips, each lasting one second.

☐ As they watch the film, their task is to try to identify as many of the moments as they can, using the present continuous tense. For example:
- ☐ *Somebody is playing a piano …*
- ☐ *A child is running …*

☐ Show the film.

☐ Get feedback, and then show the film a second time for the learners to identify more moments.

☐ Now show the film again. This time:
- ☐ Pause at each moment.
- ☐ Elicit what is happening.

☐ Ask the learners to choose five of the moments which they think are most interesting.

☐ Pair them, to explain to their partner what they find interesting about the moments they chose.

☐ Hold a plenary discussion, based on these questions:
- ☐ *What did they find interesting about the moments?*
- ☐ *How did the film make them feel?*
- ☐ *What moment would they choose, if they had to make a one-second film themselves?*

Post-production

The *Every second counts!* activities on page 87 follow on perfectly from this activity.

You can find an example of this activity here:
http://bit.ly/19WGsFd

Split-screen films

To compare two different sets of actions
in the different halves of a screen.

Pre-production

Select a 'split-screen' short film (a film where the screen
is divided into two halves, with different moving images
in each half).

For teachers who don't have time to source films themselves,
here is a link to a suitable split-screen short film:
http://bit.ly/1k64Img

Action!

☐ Tell the learners they are going to watch a split-screen
short film in which they will see different things
happening on the two halves of the screen.

☐ As they watch the film, their task is to identify similarities
and differences between the action they see on both halves
of the screen.

☐ Show the film.

☐ Pair the learners, to discuss the similarities and differences
they saw.

☐ Ask them to write five sentences, comparing what they saw
on the two halves of the screen.

☐ Play the film again.

☐ Pause at each scene, and ask the learners to discuss what
they see on both halves of the screen.

Post-production

For homework, you can ask the learners to write a short
composition comparing the actions on the 'two screens'.

You can find an example of this activity here:
http://bit.ly/TqLgvd

Infographic films

To analyse an infographic film,
and generate discussion about it.

Pre-production

Find an infographic film on YouTube or Vimeo, related to a
topic the learners are studying.

For teachers who don't have time to source films themselves,
here is a link to a suitable infographic film:
http://bit.ly/1dn65NP

Action!

☐ Elicit or explain that an 'infographic' is a graphic visual
representation of information, data or knowledge.

☐ Tell the learners they are going to watch an infographic
film:
  ▫ When they watch, their task is to note down 10 pieces
  of information or data.

☐ Play the film.

☐ The learners write 10 questions for the 10 pieces of
information or data they wrote down:
  ▫ When they are ready, pair them to ask each other their
  questions.

☐ Hold a plenary discussion:
  ▫ *What is the most interesting information or data?*
  ▫ *What is the most surprising?*
  ▫ *What is the most predictable?*

Post-production

For homework, the learners can find an infographic film
related to something they are interested in.

In the following lesson, invite them to show their films and
explain why they find them interesting.

You can find an example of this activity here:
http://bit.ly/1jLZBMc

'How to' films

To watch and listen to a film very carefully,
to be able to correct errors in a summary.

Pre-production

Select a film which you think your learners will enjoy, which shows how to do something. Two excellent websites which provide short instructional 'how to' films are:
Howcast – *http://www.howcast.com/*
Filmjug – *http://www.filmjug.com/*

Write a summary of the instructions. Change it, to include five or 10 *factual errors*, depending on the length of the film, and make copies.

For teachers who don't have time to source films themselves, here is a link to a suitable 'how to' film:
http://bit.ly/1e159vw

Action!

- ☐ Tell the learners they are going to watch a 'How to …' film:
  - ☐ *What instructions do they think they will see and hear?*

- ☐ As they watch the film, their task is to check their predictions.

- ☐ Show the film.

- ☐ Distribute your handout. Tell the learners that it is a summary of the instructions in the film.

- ☐ Explain that there are 10 factual errors. The learners' task is:
  - ☐ To watch the film again.
  - ☐ To underline the errors.
  - ☐ To write the correct information under the text.

- ☐ Show the film again.

- ☐ The learners complete the *correct* information, and then compare with a partner.

- ☐ Show the film again, and ask the learners to tell you to pause when they hear the correct information.

Post-production

For homework, the learners can find a 'how to' film which they like:
- ☐ They write a summary of the instructions, and then change it to include five or 10 factual errors, depending on the length of the film.
- ☐ They make enough copies of the summary for the class.

In the following lesson, ask a learner to distribute their summary.
- ☐ The others watch the film and underline the errors.
- ☐ They write the correct information under the text.
- ☐ In subsequent lessons, another learner does the same.

This activity procedure can be used with other types of films.

Music films

To reconstruct a story and song lyrics,
by watching a music film.

Pre-production

Select a music film which is a short film telling an interesting story. You also need a version with the lyrics displayed.

For teachers who don't have time to source films themselves, here is a link to a suitable short film:
http://bit.ly/1j8gkdQ
and a film with the song lyrics:
http://bit.ly/1pHj5CO

Action!

- ☐ Tell the learners they are going to watch, but not hear, a short film:
  - ☐ As they watch, their task is to try to remember the story the film tells.

- ☐ Play the film – with the sound *off*.

- ☐ After watching, they make some notes:
  - ☐ They try to reconstruct the story with a partner.
  - ☐ They then retell the story to the rest of the class.

- ☐ Tell the learners that the film is for a song:
  - ☐ *Can they predict the lyrics of the song?*

- ☐ Show the film – with the sound *on*:
  - ☐ The learners note down any words or expressions they understand.

- ☐ Put the learners into small groups:
  - ☐ *Can they reconstruct the lyrics?*

- ☐ Show the film again.

- ☐ Finally, show a film which displays the lyrics, for the learners to compare their lyrics with the actual lyrics.

- ☐ Hold a plenary discussion, asking the learners the following questions:
  - ☐ *Does the song have a message?*
  - ☐ *Do they think the film goes well with the lyrics of the song?*

Post-production

For homework, the learners can choose a music film of one of their favourite songs which tells a story. They watch the film several times, and then write the story the film tells.

You can find an example of this activity here:
http://bit.ly/1gVyqKC

Animated lecture films

To watch and talk about an animated video lecture.

Pre-production

Select an 'animated lecture' video (video lectures created by pairing leading experts with talented animators).

Excellent examples can be found at RSA Animate: *http://bit.ly/1nruExE*

For teachers who don't have time to source films themselves, here is a link to a suitable animated lecture video: *http://bit.ly/1pPqtih*

Action!

☐ Give the learners the subject of your animated lecture.

☐ Pair them, to discuss the following questions:
  ◌ *What do they know about the theme?*
  ◌ *What would they like to know about the theme?*

☐ Get feedback from the whole class. Write on the board:
  ◌ Some of the things they *know* about the subject.
  ◌ Some of the things they would *like* to know.

☐ Tell the learners that they are going to watch a lecture on the subject.

☐ As they watch, their task is to notice the following:
  ◌ *Are any of the things they know mentioned?*
  ◌ *Are any of the things they would like to know mentioned?*

☐ Show the video.

☐ Get feedback from the whole class.

☐ Tell the learners they are going to watch the video a second time.

☐ As they watch, their task is to tell you to pause:
  ◌ Every time there is some information they *already* know.
  ◌ Every time one of the things they *wanted* to know is mentioned.

☐ Show the video again.

☐ In small groups, the learners discuss the subject of the lecture.

Post-production

For homework, the learners can write a composition in which they give their opinion on the subject of the lecture.

You can find an example of this activity here: *http://bit.ly/U3ANq5*

Shorts on social issues

To promote discussion of a contemporary social theme.

Pre-production

Select a short film on a social theme, such as poverty, homelessness, discrimination, etc.

For teachers who don't have time to source films themselves, here is a link to a suitable short film on homelessness: *http://bit.ly/1gyRkbw*

Action!

☐ Write up the issue you're going to talk about.
  For example: *homelessness*.

☐ Pair the learners, to tell each other what they know about this issue.

☐ Hold a feedback session, and write up on the board things the learners know about the problem.

☐ Tell the learners they are going to watch a film about it.

☐ They first discuss with their partner:
  ◌ *What do they predict they will see in the film?*

☐ Show the film:
  ◌ *Were their predictions correct?*
  ◌ *How did the film make them feel?*

☐ Divide the class into groups of three and four, and dictate the following questions:
  ◌ *Is this issue a big problem in their country?*
  ◌ *What are the main causes?*
  ◌ *What can governments do to prevent it?*
  ◌ *How do they feel when they see or read about this issue?*
  ◌ *Is this problem a 'hidden' issue for their society?*

☐ The learners discuss the questions in their groups, and then you hold a plenary session on the issue.

Post-production

For homework, the learners can write a composition from the perspective of the person suffering the problem shown in the film.

There is an example of this activity here: *http://bit.ly/1d7LbUO*

You can also select a short film on another important social problem. For example, bullying; see *http://bit.ly/1lGX0AA*. Follow a similar procedure:
  ◌ *What are the most common types of bullying?*
  ◌ *What do they predict they will see in the film?*
  ◌ *Were their predictions correct?*

There is an example of this activity here: *http://bit.ly/Kq7XuD*

Chapter Two
Actively producing

Chapter Two offers guidance on what may seem a radical departure: to get learners to produce their own moving image texts inside the classroom and beyond.

We have already suggested – when we looked at the changing nature of literacy in the 21st century – that young people need to be able to 'read' and 'write' in *all* forms of communication, not just the written word.

Asking the learners to create their own short films and videos is a very effective way to engage them in active learning:

- Producing moving images is intrinsically motivating for learners.
- It helps them develop the types of skills which are in demand in the modern-day workplace.
- It foments collaboration, decision-making and creativity.

Expensive equipment is no longer needed to make a film – the learners can create very good short films with a mobile phone or tablet. They can also edit them, using a mobile device or computer. Moving image creation can be done in class, as the main activity, or at home, as a follow-up activity.

My life – the movie

The learners write about their lives.

Pre-production

Select a biopic which you have enjoyed, and find a trailer of it.

For teachers who don't have time to source films themselves, here is a link to a suitable trailer: *http://bit.ly/JwjkBc*

Action!

☐ Write *Biopic* on the board. Elicit or explain that a biopic is a biographical film.

☐ Tell the learners about a biopic *you* liked, and why you enjoyed it.

☐ Tell them they are going to watch the trailer of the biopic:
- *What do they expect to be shown in the trailer?*

☐ Show the trailer of the biopic:
- *What do they expect to be shown in the film?*

☐ Pair the learners, to think of a biopic *they* have enjoyed:
- They discuss it with their partner.

☐ Tell them to imagine that a famous film director wants to make a film of their life.

☐ They choose the following:
- The director
- An actor to play their role
- Actors to play other roles
- The setting

☐ Now invite them to write down three scenes they would like to see included in the film:
- You set a time limit of 10 minutes.
- You walk round, providing help with language as necessary.

☐ When the learners are ready, put them into pairs to compare their biopics.

☐ Round off with a whole-class discussion on their films.

Post-production

For homework, the learners can write the film script for one of the scenes.

Acknowledgement

This activity is adapted from an activity in *Being Creative* by Chaz Pugliese (Delta).

My town

Using film to generate writing, discussing – and filming.

Pre-production

Find old film footage of the town where you are living.

Action!

☐ Ask the learners if their home town, or the town they are currently living in, has changed a lot in the last 100 years.

☐ Pair them, to discuss the changes. Encourage them to use constructions such as:
- *There was …*
- *There were …*
- *There used to be …*
- *There didn't used to be …*

☐ Tell the learners that they are going to watch film footage of the town:
- *What differences do they notice between the town then and the town now?*

☐ Show the film.

☐ The learners write a narrative on the differences. Again, encourage them to use the same constructions:
- *There was …*
- *There were …*
- *There used to be …*
- *There didn't used to be …*

☐ Set a time limit of five minutes.

☐ Pair the learners, to compare their narratives.

☐ Hold a plenary session, to discuss how the town has changed.

Post-production

For homework, the learners can film on a mobile device a part of town:
- They choose a street, a building, a monument, etc, which is important to them.
- They film it for about one minute.

In the following lesson, they bring their mobile device to class and show their video to a partner, explaining why that part of town is important to them.

My poem

Writing a poem from the visual clues in a short film.

Pre-production

Find a video which is a visual representation of a poem.

For teachers who don't have time to source films themselves, here is a link to a suitable video:
http://bit.ly/1cFnrpc

Action!

☐ Ask the learners what their favourite poem is.

☐ Give them the first line of *your* poem, and ask them to discuss it.

☐ Tell them they are going to *watch*, but not *hear*, a video which is a visual representation of the poem.

☐ Show the video without sound.

☐ Invite the learners to write a poem based on the images they see in the film. You can show it as many times as necessary:
  ◌ You set a time limit of 10 minutes.
  ◌ You walk round, providing help with language as necessary.

☐ Ask the learners to read their poem to a partner.

☐ Then invite them to read out their poems to the rest of the class.

☐ Show the video *with* sound.

☐ The learners compare their poems with the original.

Post-production

For homework, you can ask the learners to work more on their poem and create a more polished version.

You can see an example of this activity here:
http://bit.ly/JrWAC7

My favourite scene

Describing a film scene.

Pre-production

Prepare a description of one of your favourite film scenes, using the present tense. Try to make the description as vivid as possible. Do not use the name of the film, or the names of any of the characters.

Action!

☐ Tell the learners you are going to describe one of your favourite film scenes:
  ◌ *Can they guess what film you are describing?*

☐ Read out your description.

☐ Elicit the title of the film:
  ◌ If they can't guess correctly, they can ask questions in order to find out.

☐ Show the scene:
  ◌ *Do they think your description was a good one?*

☐ Tell the learners their task is to think of one of *their* favourite film scenes:
  ◌ They should write a paragraph, describing it as vividly as possible.
  ◌ They should use the present tense, and as much descriptive language as possible.

☐ Set a time limit of 10 minutes and walk round, providing help with language – especially descriptive adjectives.

☐ Divide the class into groups of three or four:
  ◌ Each learner describes their favourite scene.
  ◌ The others have to guess it.

☐ If they don't know the scene, they ask questions to find out.

Post-production

For homework, you can get the learners to write a more polished version of the description of their film scene.

Looks interesting

The learners create a narrative, based on visual clues.

Pre-production

Select a short film which has a clear storyline – but no dialogue.

For teachers who don't have time to source films themselves, here is a link to a suitable video:
http://bit.ly/1nXNX1Q

Action!

☐ Write the title of your film on the board. Tell the learners they are going to watch a short film with this title:
   ☐ *What do they think they will see in the film?*

☐ Get feedback from the whole class on what they think they will see.

☐ Show the film:
   ☐ The learners' task is to compare their predictions with the story told.

☐ Divide the class into groups of three or four.

☐ Show the film again:
   ☐ The learners' task is to summarise the events, and create a narrative.

☐ The learners collaborate on creating the narrative:
   ☐ You set a time limit of 10 minutes.
   ☐ You walk round, providing help with language as necessary.

☐ A member of each group reads out their narrative, for the other learners to comment.

☐ Show the film one more time, for the learners to discuss the film and the various narratives.

Post-production

For homework, the learners can write a narrative based on the story the film tells, but with an alternative ending.

You can do a similar activity, this time with the learners speculating starting from *the opening scene*.

You can also select a film with an especially *intriguing* title, for the learners to predict what the film is going to be about. For example:
The Adventures of a Cardboard Box
My Shoes
Love is Like Life but Longer

The learners can bring *their own* intriguing film titles to class for a prediction activity.

You can find an example of this activity here:
http://bit.ly/1A00WVP

Sounds interesting

The learners write a narrative, based on audio clues.

Pre-production

Select a short film or clip with little or no dialogue. Prepare the following questions for the learners:
☐ *How many people are in the film?*
☐ *Where is the film set?*
☐ *What sounds can you hear?*
☐ *What is happening?*
☐ *What images do you think you are going to see in the film?*

Teachers who don't have time to source films for themselves will find a link to a suitable film clip here:
http://bit.ly/JybLtw

Action!

☐ Tell the learners they are going to *hear*, but not *see*, a short film or clip.

☐ Write your questions on the board:
   ☐ Tell the learners that they should answer them as they listen to the film.

☐ Play the film, with no vision.

☐ The learners compare their answers with a partner. Encourage them to use the language of speculation. For example:
   ☐ *It might be …*
   ☐ *It must be …*
   ☐ *It can't be …*

☐ Go through the questions, and write up the learners' answers.

☐ Divide the class into groups of three or four:
   ☐ They write the narrative of the film, using the present simple tense.
   ☐ Their narrative should have a clear beginning, middle and end.

☐ You set a time limit of 10 minutes and walk round, helping with language as necessary:
   ☐ The learners then explain their narrative to a member of another group.

☐ You show the film with sound *and* vision:
   ☐ The learners compare *their* narratives with the story shown in the film.

Post-production

For homework, the learners can write a composition based on the story told in the film.

A dramatic pursuit

Describing a chase scene.

Pre-production

Select a dramatic chase scene.

Teachers who don't have time to source films for themselves will find a link to a suitable film clip here:
http://bit.ly/1ix8Opn

Action!

☐ Elicit or explain that a chase scene is a typical scene in an action movie where one car pursues another:
  ☐ *Can the learners think of any famous movie chase scenes?*

☐ Tell them they are going to view a chase scene and, as they watch, they should think about the following questions:
  ☐ *Who is chasing who?*
  ☐ *Why?*
  ☐ *Where?*
  ☐ *When?*
  ☐ *How?*
  ☐ *How fast?*
  ☐ *What is the result?*

☐ Show the scene twice.

☐ Pair the learners, to answer the questions:
  ☐ They reconstruct the chase.
  ☐ They use the present tense and prepositions of place and movement.

☐ Set a time limit of 10 minutes and walk round, helping with language as necessary.

☐ When the learners are ready, ask them to compare their reconstruction with another pair.

☐ Divide the class into groups of three or four:
  ☐ They have to create *their own* chase scene.
  ☐ They have to use the present tense and prepositions of place and movement.

☐ Now suggest the following:
  ☐ They divide the scene into four phases.
  ☐ They heighten the drama with narrow escapes.

☐ Set a time limit of 15 minutes and walk round, helping with language as necessary.

☐ The learners read out their chases, for the rest of the class to comment.

Post-production

For homework, the learners can write more polished and more extensive versions of their chase scenes.

A dramatic incident

Writing a police report.

Pre-production

Select a film clip which shows a scene of a dramatic event, such as:
- ☐ A robbery   ☐ An attempted suicide
- ☐ A crime   ☐ An attempted kidnapping

Teachers who don't have time to source films for themselves will find a link to a suitable film clip here:
http://bit.ly/1lIJtLM

Action!

☐ Write *Dramatic incident* on the board, and elicit examples from the class:
  ☐ Tell the learners that they are going to watch a dramatic incident on film.

☐ As they watch, they will have to do the following:
  ☐ They imagine that they are police officers who were involved in the incident.
  ☐ They will then write a report to a superior officer, explaining what happened in the incident.
  ☐ They should be very observant, as they will only see it once!

☐ In their report, they should answer some of the following questions:
  ☐ *How did it start?*
  ☐ *What events happened, and in what order?*
  ☐ *How did it end?*

☐ Play the film.

☐ The learners work on their reports individually:
  ☐ You set a time limit of 10 minutes.
  ☐ You walk round, providing help with language as necessary.

☐ They compare their reports with a partner.

☐ Hold a feedback session on the reports, and discuss any doubts the learners have.

☐ Show the film a second time, to clarify their doubts.

Post-production

For homework, the learners can write an extended incident report.

Alternatively, they can find another film clip which shows a dramatic scene and write an extended report about that.

Acknowledgement

This activity is adapted from one in *Images* by Jamie Keddie (OUP).

From text to film

The learners create a film script,
starting from a written text.

Pre-production

Choose a passage from a novel, short story or graded reader which is suitable for the level of your learners and which has been made into a film. Make copies of the text and prepare the film adaptation.

Action!

☐ Tell the learners to imagine that they are scriptwriters who are writing a film adaptation of a novel:
  ☐ Their task will be to write a script, based on the text you are going to give them,

☐ Go through the scriptwriting conventions checklist from *Scrutinising a script* on page 63:
  ☐ The learners' task will be to follow the conventions, so that their script looks like a film script.

☐ Pair the learners, give them the text and ask them to discuss it:
  ☐ Give them 15 minutes to write their scripts.
  ☐ Monitor and help them follow the conventions.

☐ When the learners are ready, each group performs their script in front of the rest of the class.

☐ Show the film adaptation of the scene.

☐ Get the learners to compare *their* scripts with the film adaptation.

Post-production

For homework, the learners can choose a scene from one of their favourite books:
  ☐ They use the scriptwriting conventions.
  ☐ They write a film adaptation of the scene.

They can also choose the actors they would like to appear in the film.

From seeing to doing

The learners write a script for a 'how to' video,
starting by seeing one.

Pre-production

Select a video which you think your learners will enjoy, which shows how to do something. Two excellent websites which provide instructional 'how to' videos are:
Howcast – *http://www.howcast.com/*
Videojug – *http://www.videojug.com/*

For teachers who don't have time to source films themselves, here is a link to a suitable 'how to' video:
http://bit.ly/1dEByur

Action!

☐ Tell the learners they are going to watch a video entitled 'How to …':
  ☐ *What instructions do they think they will see and hear?*

☐ Tell them that they are going to *watch*, but not *hear*, the video:
  ☐ As they watch, they have to imagine what the person giving the instructions is saying.

☐ Play the video twice without sound.

☐ Divide the class into groups of three or four.

☐ Their task is to write a script for the video, in which they describe clearly how to do the action:
  ☐ You set a time limit of 10 minutes .
  ☐ You walk round, helping with language as necessary.

☐ Each group comes to the front of the class, and reads out their script – while you play the video.

☐ Now play the video *with* sound, for the learners to compare their scripts with the original.

Post-production

For homework, the learners can find a 'how to' video which explains something they think is useful:
  ☐ They watch it several times, and write a summary of the instructions.

In the following lesson, you ask a learner to play their video with no sound:
  ☐ The others write the script for the video.
  ☐ The learner who has chosen the video helps them with vocabulary.

In subsequent lessons, you ask other learners to follow the same procedure.

Alternatively, the learners can choose a 'how to' video which they enjoy. They watch it several times, make notes and then write a summary of how to do the action.

From sky to screen

The learners reconstruct a script,
starting from a word cloud.

Pre-production

A word cloud is a visual representation of words in a text to
show relative frequency. Select a word cloud generating site.
Two excellent choices are:

Wordle – *http://www.wordle.net/*
Tagxedo – *http://www.tagxedo.com/*

Choose a short video which has an interesting voice-over.
Find or make a transcript of the video. Enter the transcript
into either Wordle or Tagxedo, to create a word cloud.

Action!

☐ Introduce the theme of the video you are going to watch.

☐ Show the learners the word cloud you created from the
transcript of the video:
- They can use a dictionary to look up the words they
don't know.

☐ Tell them they are going to watch a short video in which
the words from the word cloud appear:
- *What do they think they will see and hear in the video?*

☐ Tell them they are going to *watch*, but not *hear*, the film:
- As they watch, they will imagine the script for the video.

☐ Play the film with no sound.

☐ Pair the learners and ask them to write the script of the
voice-over for the film:
- They use the vocabulary in the word cloud.
- You set a time limit of 10 minutes.

☐ Tell them that you are going to show the video again
with *no sound*:
- Each pair takes turns coming to the front of the class.
- They read their voice-over as they watch the film.

☐ Comment on each pair's voice-over.

☐ Show the learners the video *with sound*, and compare
their voice-overs with the original.

Post-production

For homework, you can give the learners the transcript of
the video:
- They read the script aloud several times and then
video themselves.
- They send you a video file.

You watch their voice-over and give them feedback on it.

You can see an example of this activity here:
http://bit.ly/1kekbXl

From subtitle to subtitle

Translating subtitles into English,
and comparing them to the originals.

Pre-production

This activity is only appropriate for monolingual classes:
- Select a DVD which has subtitles in your learners'
language, and choose a short scene which has interesting
dialogue.
- Select the subtitles of the learners' L1.

Action!

☐ Tell the learners they are going to watch a scene from a
film with subtitles in their language, but they will not *hear*
the film:
- As they watch, their task is to write down the subtitles.

☐ Play the film clip twice with no sound for the learners to
compare their answers in pairs.

☐ Show the film again, pausing at each subtitle, for the
learners to check they have the correct subtitles.

☐ Divide the class into small groups:
- They have 10 minutes to translate the subtitles into
English.

☐ Now show the clip with subtitles in English:
- The learners watch the clip.
- They compare the subtitles with their translations.

☐ Show the clip with sound *and* subtitles in English.

☐ Hold a feedback session on the difference between the
original translation and the original subtitles in English.

Post-production

For homework, the learners can choose a DVD in English
which they have at home:
- They choose a scene, watch it in English with subtitles
in their language, and translate the subtitles into English.
- They watch the film again, this time with the subtitles
in English, and compare these to *their* translated subtitles.

For homework, you can ask the learners to go to a website
like ClipFlair, and write English subtitles:
http://clipflair.net/

They can also subtitle and dub videos at Bombay TV, which
has a collection of very short Indian film clips and a space
to add three lines of subtitles:
http://www.grapheine.com/bombaytv/

Food for thought

Imagining a 'thought script' for a short silent film.

Pre-production

Select a short film or clip which has two main characters, but no dialogue.

Teachers who don't have time to source films for themselves will find a link to a suitable short film here: *http://bit.ly/1ayKVZs*

Action!

☐ Tell the learners that they are going to watch a short film which has no dialogue:
  - ▫ *What do they imagine the two main characters are thinking at key moments throughout the film?*

☐ Show the film.

☐ Draw a thought bubble on the board.

☐ Pair the learners, and assign them one of the two main characters each:
  - ▫ They should watch the film again, and write a 'thought script' of what their character is thinking at key moments during the film.
  - ▫ They should draw a 'thought bubble' for their character at those moments, and complete it with the characters' thoughts.

☐ Show the film again:
  - ▫ Pause at key moments, to give the learners time to write down what their character is thinking.

☐ When they are ready, ask them to roleplay their scripts.

☐ Show the film a third time:
  - ▫ Pause at key moments again, for the learners to read out and discuss their characters' thoughts.

Post-production

For homework, the learners can write a letter from the perspective of their character to the other character.

You can see an example of this activity here: *http://bit.ly/1gVyqKC*

Take it from here

The learners talk about sequels – and then create one.

Pre-production

Choose a short film which has a simple narrative with a clear beginning, middle and end.

Teachers who don't have time to source films for themselves will find a link to a suitable short film here: *http://bit.ly/19zmTCA*

Action!

☐ Write *Sequel* on the board:
  - ▫ Elicit or explain that it is a film which continues a story which began in another film.

☐ Put the learners into small groups, to explain to their partners any films they like which have a sequel or sequels:
  - ▫ *What makes a successful sequel?*

☐ Tell the learners that they are going to watch a short film, and that they will have to answer the following questions:
  - ▫ *What story does the film tell?*
  - ▫ *Is it a convincing story?*
  - ▫ *What are the main characters like?*
  - ▫ *Do they like the main characters?*

☐ Play the film:
  - ▫ The learners discuss their answers in their groups.

☐ Tell them they are going to watch the film again:
  - ▫ Their task is now to write a sequel to the film.

☐ Show the film a second time:
  - ▫ The groups have 15 minutes to write their sequel.

☐ When they are ready, ask one volunteer from each group to read their sequel aloud, for the others to comment on the stories.

☐ Hold a vote:
  - ▫ *Which is the best sequel?*
  - ▫ *The funniest?*
  - ▫ *The most original?*

Post-production

For homework, you can ask the learners to write a 'prequel' (a film that tells the part of a story that happened *before* the story in another film).

Storyboard

To imagine how a written text might be filmed, and represent the ideas visually on a storyboard.

Pre-production

Select a short scene from a novel, short story or graded reader. Make enough copies of both the text and a storyboard template for the class. Find examples of these types of camera shots:

LS – *long shot*   CU – *close-up*
MS – *mid shot*   Z – *zoom in*
HCA/LCA – *high/low camera angle*

Action!

☐ Divide the class into groups of three or four, and distribute the storyboards.

☐ Elicit or explain:
   ☐ Storyboards are graphic representations that film-makers use to create picture outlines of scenes in a film.
   ☐ Each frame illustrates a point in the story, and the space under each frame is used for writing a short description of the action, the dialogue, camera shots and angles, sound effects and music.

☐ Explain or review different kinds of camera shots and their abbreviations. See above.

☐ Check the learners' understanding, by showing examples of each type of shot.

☐ Distribute the texts.

☐ The learners' task is:
   ☐ To read the text and decide how they would represent the text on film.
   ☐ To break the text up into important points.
   ☐ To use the storyboards to decide what would appear in each frame in a film adaptation of the text.
   ☐ To include very brief notes on the action, dialogue, camera shots and angles, and any sound effects and music.

☐ In their groups, the learners discuss their ideas and complete their storyboards:
   ☐ You set a time limit of 15 minutes.

☐ The groups take turns presenting their storyboards and telling their story visually to another group.

☐ Conduct a feedback session, based on the visual stories in the storyboards.

Post-production

If the text the learners read has been adapted to a film, you can show the relevant scene and compare it with the learners' visual stories.

Storyboard

☐ Camera position ☐ What is happening ☐ What is being said ☐ Sound effects/music	☐ Camera position ☐ What is happening ☐ What is being said ☐ Sound effects/music	☐ Camera position ☐ What is happening ☐ What is being said ☐ Sound effects/music
☐ Camera position ☐ What is happening ☐ What is being said ☐ Sound effects/music	☐ Camera position ☐ What is happening ☐ What is being said ☐ Sound effects/music	☐ Camera position ☐ What is happening ☐ What is being said ☐ Sound effects/music

My film – my poster

The learners imagine a film, create a poster for it
and present the film.

Pre-production

Find a poster of a film you think your learners will like.
Choose a website where they can create beautiful posters.
A good choice is:
http://glogster.com

You will need a computer, data-projector and screen
for this activity.

The activity also requires one computer per learner.

Action!

☐ Project the image of your movie poster onto the screen:
  ◦ *What information does the poster give about the film?*

☐ Try to elicit the following information, and write it on the
board in the form of a chart:

Name of the film	
Names of actors	
Slogan or catch-phrase	
Première date	
Favourable reviews	
Award nominations	

☐ Pair the learners, to think of a film they would like to make.

☐ Invite them to complete the chart you have written on
the board with information about their film.

☐ When the learners are ready, give them the address of
the website (see above):
  ◦ They create their own film posters.
  ◦ They use the answers in their chart, and images
    from Google.

☐ You set a time limit of 15 minutes and walk round,
providing help with language as necessary.

☐ When they are ready, each pair in turn displays their
poster and gives a short presentation about their film.

Post-production

The learners imagine that they are the publicists for the film,
and write a press release for it – they should obviously make
the film sound as attractive as possible.

Acknowledgement

This activity is adapted from an activity in *Digital Play*
by Kyle Mawer and Graham Stanley (Delta).

My film – my presentation

Preparing a PechaKucha presentation
on a favourite film.

Pre-production

Prepare a PechaKucha of one of your favourite films,
using images. You can use this video, which explains what
a PechaKucha is:
http://bit.ly/1bz4xvy

Make copies of the description of different types of shots
in *Camera shots* on page 35.

Action!

☐ Write *PechaKucha* on the board:
  ◦ *Do the learners know what it means?*

☐ If they don't know, tell them:
  ◦ It is a presentation of 20 slides.
  ◦ Each slide is presented in 20 seconds.
  ◦ This means the presentation lasts six minutes and
    40 seconds.

☐ Show the PechaKucha video, which explains what a
PechaKucha is.

☐ Tell the learners that you are going to give a PechaKucha
presentation of one of your favourite films.

☐ Give the presentation:
  ◦ Invite the learners to ask you questions about the film.

☐ Tell the learners that, for homework, you want them to
prepare their own PechaKucha presentation on one of
their favourite films. It should include:
  ◦ Main characters
  ◦ Close-up
  ◦ Mid shot
  ◦ Long shot

☐ If your learners don't understand the different types
of shots, give them a copy of the handout with the
description.

☐ The learners prepare their presentation at home.

☐ In the following lesson, they take turns presenting their
PechaKucha.

☐ After each presentation, they ask the speaker-presenter
questions about their favourite film.

Post-production

You can use PechaKucha presentations on favourite books,
favourite cities, best holidays, etc.

My life – the soundtrack

The learners imagine a film of their life,
and compile the soundtrack.

Pre-production

Choose a biopic that you like, and think of reasons why you like it.

Also, choose three songs you would include in a soundtrack of the biopic of *your* life. They should be songs that were important to you at different stages of your life.

Action!

☐ Write *Biopic* on the board:
- ☐ Elicit or explain that it is a biographical film.

☐ Tell the learners about a biopic you liked, and why you enjoyed it.

☐ Pair the learners:
- ☐ They think of a biopic *they* have enjoyed.
- ☐ They discuss it with their partner.

☐ Tell them that a famous film director wants to make a film of their life.

☐ Ask them to choose:
- ☐ The director
- ☐ An actor to play their role
- ☐ Actors to play other roles
- ☐ The setting

☐ Now tell them they are going to choose three songs, to be included in the soundtrack of the film:
- ☐ The songs should be important in their lives.

☐ Tell the learners the three songs that you would include in the soundtrack of *your* biopic:
- ☐ Explain why they are important to *you*.

☐ They choose *their* three songs, and write brief notes on why each song is important in their life:
- ☐ You set a time limit of 10 minutes.
- ☐ You walk round, providing help with language as necessary.

☐ When the learners are ready, put them into pairs:
- ☐ They explain the three songs they have chosen.
- ☐ They explain why they are important to them.

☐ Hold a whole-class discussion on their soundtracks.

Post-production

For homework, you can ask the learners to compile the entire soundtrack of the film of their life, with a brief explanation of why they chose each song.

A suitable soundtrack

The learners imagine they are producing
a film adaptation of a text.

Pre-production

Select a passage from a novel, short story or graded reader.

Make enough copies of the text, and prepare to show the scene, if there a film adaptation.

Action!

☐ Ask the learners to tell a partner about their favourite film soundtrack:
- ☐ *Why do they like it so much?*

☐ Set a time limit of four minutes.

☐ Tell the learners they are going to read a short text.

☐ Distribute the text:
- ☐ They have to imagine that they are the producer making a film adaptation of the text they are going to read.
- ☐ They have to find songs and musical accompaniment that go well with the story.

☐ The learners read the text:
- ☐ They have to visualise the written text, and what song or type of music would suit the story.
- ☐ They have to give reasons to support their decision.

☐ Pair the learners, to explain their choice to their partner.

☐ Conduct a feedback session, based on the soundtracks.

☐ If the text the learners read has already been adapted to film:
- ☐ Show the relevant scene.
- ☐ Listen to the music.
- ☐ Compare it with *their* soundtrack.

Post-production

For homework, you can ask the learners to compile an entire soundtrack for a short story, novel or graded reader they have enjoyed:
- ☐ They add a brief explanation of why they chose each song or piece of music.

They prepare a 'mixtape' – a compilation of their soundtrack – and share it with you and the other learners.

A natural voice-over

Creating a script to accompany the images
in a nature documentary.

Pre-production

Choose a two-minute film clip from a nature documentary.

Teachers who don't have time to source films for themselves
will find a link to a suitable film clip here:
http://bit.ly/1v1iOQe

Action!

☐ Write *Voice-over* on the board, and elicit or explain that
it is the narrative spoken by a person who is not seen
in a film:
  ▫ *What types of film usually have a voice-over?*

☐ The learners will probably answer: documentaries.

☐ Tell the class that they are going to watch a short clip
from a nature documentary:
  ▫ In groups of three, their task is to write the script for
  a voice-over to go with the images.

☐ Play the film clip, with the sound turned *off*:
  ▫ The learners discuss their ideas for the soundtrack,
  and write a voice-over to go with it.

☐ Point out:
  ▫ It may be very difficult to describe everything they see
  in the clip.
  ▫ It may be best to concentrate on the main events.

☐ Show the clip several times, giving the learners time to
complete their scripts.

☐ When they are ready, ask a volunteer from each group
to read their script aloud – while you show the film
with the sound *off*.

☐ Hold a plenary discussion:
  ▫ *Which script was the best/most original?*
  ▫ *What did the learners find difficult about writing the
  script?*

☐ Finally, show the film clip with the sound *on*, for the
learners to compare their scripts with the original
soundtrack.

Post-production

The learners can find a clip from a documentary on a subject
they are interested in:
  ▫ They watch with the sound off, and write their voice-over.
  ▫ They can read the script aloud several times, and then
  video themselves.

They send you the video file, you watch the video and give
feedback on content, presentation and pronunciation.

A trailer voice-over

Writing the script to go with a film presentation.

Pre-production

Find a film trailer you think your learners will like
at a website such as:
  ▫ Yahoo Movies – *http://movies.yahoo.com*
  ▫ Apple Trailers – *http://apple.com/trailers/*
  ▫ Coming Soon – *http://www.comingsoon.net/trailers/*

Action!

☐ Write the word *Trailer* on the board.

☐ Elicit or explain that a trailer is a short filmed
advertisement for a feature-length film:
  ▫ *What do you usually see and hear in a trailer?*

☐ Tell them they are going to *see*, but not *hear*, a film trailer.

☐ Their task is to write down important information:
  ▫ The plot
  ▫ The characters
  ▫ The actors

☐ Show the trailer.

☐ The learners compare with a partner the information
they have written down.

☐ Divide the class into groups of three or four, to prepare
a script for a voice-over of the trailer:
  ▫ You set a time limit of 10 minutes.
  ▫ You walk round, providing help with language as
  necessary.

☐ The learners give their voice-over, while you show the
trailer with no sound.

☐ They comment on each other's voice-overs.

☐ Show the trailer with the sound *on*:
  ▫ The learners compare the original with *their* voice-overs.

Post-production

For homework, the learners can go to one of the trailer sites:
  ▫ They watch a number of trailers for current films.
  ▫ They choose the film they would most like to see.

In the following lesson, the learners say which film they would
like to see, and why.

Revoice!

The learners engage in the experience
of revoicing a video.

Pre-production

Choose a website that allows the learners to 'revoice' short
film clips (to add speech to a clip, such as voice-over,
dubbing, respeaking, audio description, free commentary,
karaoke singing and reciting).

ClipFlair is an excellent choice:
http://clipflair.net/
Watch a one-minute tutorial on how to use ClipFlair:
http://bit.ly/1f0PF19
Look at the Gallery, which showcases revoicing activities:
http://gallery.clipflair.net/activity/

This activity requires one computer per pair of learners.

Action!

☐ Tell the learners they are going to revoice a video:
   ▫ You explain what this involves.

☐ Show the one-minute tutorial on how to use ClipFlair:
   ▫ Alternatively, the learners can go to ClipFlair
     (*http://clipflair.net/*) – and click on 'Watch 1 intro to
     Clip+Flair'.

☐ When they have finished watching, tell them to click on
  'Create activities with ClipFlair Studio':
   ▫ A player appears, with a video with captions.
   ▫ The learners' task is to read the captions and record
     themselves.

☐ To record their voice, they just click on the round red
  button ('Record Audio') and start speaking.

☐ The learners finish reading and recording themselves:
   ▫ To listen to themselves, they press the green button
     ('Play Audio').
   ▫ To save their work, they click on the 'Save' button at the
     bottom of the activity window.

☐ They can share their file, sending it by email or posting it
  to ClipFlair Social Network: *http://social.clipflair.net/*

☐ Ask the learners to send you the file:
   ▫ You listen to it and give them feedback on their
     pronunciation.

Post-production

The learners can revoice more videos by going to the
ClipFlair Gallery and selecting a video.

Alternatively, *you* can choose an activity from the ClipFlair
Gallery – or create *your own* with the Studio – for the
learners to do.

Dialogue dubbing

The learners write a short dialogue,
then subtitle and dub a short film scene.

Pre-production

Choose a website that allows you to subtitle and dub videos.
A good choice is Bombay TV, which has a collection of
Indian film clips – each clip is very short, and has a space to
add three lines of subtitles:
http://www.grapheine.com/bombaytv/

This activity requires one computer per pair of learners.

Action!

☐ Sitting at their computers, tell the learners to go to
  Bombay TV.

☐ Pair the learners, to choose a video which they like:
   ▫ They select a movie and watch it.

☐ Tell them that they are going to invent and write the
  subtitles for the movie:
   ▫ They add their subtitles to the video.

☐ When they are ready, they watch each other's videos.

☐ Now turn off the sound:
   ▫ The learners take turns.
   ▫ They say their words in real time, dubbing the video
     as it plays.

☐ Next, they read and record their dialogues:
   ▫ They send you a link to the video.

☐ In the following lesson, you can show the learners the
  dubbed videos:
   ▫ *Can they guess who dubbed which video?*

☐ Hold a vote for the best/funniest/silliest dubbed dialogue.

Post-production

The learners can also create similar subtitled or dubbed
videos at B Movie TV:
http://bit.ly/Knjr2J

They can create subtitled or dubbed football videos here:
http://bit.ly/1i28zCx

Linking up

Creating an interactive image, with links to videos
about the learners' favourite films.

Pre-production

Ask the learners to bring a photo of themselves to the
following lesson. Choose a tool that provides users with the
ability to turn any image into an interactive graphic, such as
Thinglink: *http://www.thinglink.com/*

Here is a tutorial video which shows you how to use
Thinglink: *http://bit.ly/1CoPGr5*

This activity requires one computer per pair of learners.

Action!

- ☐ Tell the learners to think about:
  - ◌ Their favourite film
  - ◌ Their favourite film scene
  - ◌ Their favourite actor
  - ◌ Their favourite soundtrack
- ☐ Pair them, to tell their partner.
- ☐ Tell them they are now going to create an interactive
  image, based on this information:
  - ◌ Show them the tutorial on how to use Thinglink.
- ☐ With the learners at their computers, give them the
  address: *http://www.thinglink.com/*.
- ☐ Tell them to click on the 'Create' button and then upload
  the photo of themselves they have brought to class:
  - ◌ When they have uploaded the image, they will have to
    create links to videos which give more information
    about their favourite film, scene, actor and soundtrack.
- ☐ Tell them to look on YouTube for videos which give
  interesting information, and then create the links to their
  images:
  - ◌ When they have finished adding the video links to their
    images, they give their image an appropriate name and
    then send you a link.
- ☐ In the following lesson, each learner shows and explains
  their image:
  - ◌ They talk about their favourite film, scene, actor and
    soundtrack.
- ☐ They can also play the videos, to give further information
  about their cinema favourites.

Post-production

Thinglink can also be used for learners to get to know each
other – by creating a link to videos about favourite music,
hobbies, maps with places they have lived in or visited,
favourite song, band or singer, etc.

I am what I am ... or am I?

You and your learners create videos
– with a twist.

Pre-production

Write a script in which you introduce yourself to your
learners – telling them some interesting facts about your life,
but also including three pieces of information which are not
true.

Action!

- ☐ Introduce yourself to your learners, reciting your script
  from memory:
  - ◌ Tell them that three pieces of information are *not true*.
- ☐ Pair the learners, to discuss which pieces of information
  might be false.
- ☐ Ask the learners if they know different ways of creating
  videos. Elicit or explain ways of creating a video:
  - ◌ Using a webcam on a computer.
  - ◌ Using a mobile phone or tablet.
  - ◌ Using a digital camera.
  - ◌ Using a camcorder.
- ☐ Discuss as a whole class.
- ☐ For homework, the learners create videos – using one of
  the techniques you discussed – in which *they* introduce
  themselves:
  - ◌ They explain some interesting things about their life.
  - ◌ They include three false pieces of information.
- ☐ Ask them to upload their videos to YouTube, to share them
  with the class.
- ☐ In the following lesson:
  - ◌ They watch each other's videos and attempt to identify
    the false pieces of information.
  - ◌ You give them feedback on their scripts and
    presentation.

Post-production

The learners can also create videos in which they talk about
their tastes in films and actors – again, they include three
false pieces of information

In the next lesson, they watch each other's videos and try to
identify the false pieces of information.

Every second counts!

Creating and compiling very short videos.

One-second films

Pre-production

Select a video which is a compilation of one-second-long videos – here is a link to a suitable compilation video: *http://bit.ly/1p7vsbf*

You can see an example of this activity here: *http://bit.ly/19WGsFd*

Action!

☐ Tell the learners they are going to watch a compilation of very short videos:
  ☐ As they watch, they should try to remember as many of the 'moments' as they can.

☐ Show the film.

☐ Ask the learners to call out the moments they remember.

☐ Tell them that they should imagine they are film-makers taking part in a 'One-second film competition':
  ☐ They should record a second of something beautiful, important or moving for them.
  ☐ They can use any digital format: digital camera, mobile phone, tablet or camcorder.
  ☐ They should bring their 'moment' to the next lesson.

☐ In the following lesson, put the students into small groups:
  ☐ They show their films.
  ☐ They explain why they chose this moment to the others.

☐ Ask the learners to vote on the best/most original/most beautiful film.

Five-second videos

Pre-production

Using a mobile device, record a five-second clip of something which is important to you in your everyday life.

Action!

☐ Show the class your five-second clip, and explain why it is important for you.

☐ Pair the learners:
  ☐ They tell their partner about a normal day in their life.

☐ Ask them to share something in their everyday life with the rest of the class:
  ☐ Something which is important to them.
  ☐ Something they enjoy.
  ☐ Something interesting or beautiful.

☐ Tell them that you want them to record a five-second clip of something related to their daily life:
  ☐ They do this every day – for five days.

☐ After a week, ask the learners to send you the five files:
  ☐ Alternatively, they share them on a file-sharing site such as Dropbox.

☐ Create a video compilation of their videos, using video-editing software such as Windows Movie Maker or Apple iMovie.

☐ Show the learners the video:
  ☐ They comment on the things which are important to them in their daily lives.

Sixty-second descriptions

Pre-production

Prepare a one-minute description of one of your favourite actors.

Action!

☐ Tell the learners about your favourite actor:
  ☐ *Is there any additional information they would like to know?*

☐ Tell the learners that their task is to create a one-minute-long description of one of *their* favourite actors:
  ☐ You set a time limit of 10 minutes.
  ☐ You walk round, providing help with language as necessary.
  ☐ They practise reading their descriptions aloud several times.

☐ In pairs, they film each other performing their descriptions on a mobile phone or other mobile device.

☐ Finally, ask the learners to upload their videos to YouTube – you share them with all the class, and encourage the learners to comment on each other's descriptions.

Post-production

☐ As a longer-term project, the learners can record two-second videos of things which are beautiful or important for them – every day for thirty days.
  ☐ Each learner creates their own 60-second compilation.
  ☐ They upload their videos to YouTube.

☐ They show the videos to the rest of the class, and explain the reasons for their choices.

Filming a letter

The learners record a visual letter
to send to a friend or relative.

Pre-production

Select a 'video letter' (a form of communication in which
a person sends another person information in the form of
moving images and sound, instead of written text).

For teachers who don't have time to source films themselves,
here is a link to a suitable video letter:
http://bit.ly/1kSNfmF

Action!

☐ Ask the learners what information a personal letter
  normally contains.

☐ Tell them they are going to watch a 'video letter' in which
  a person gives personal news and information:
  ▫ As they watch, their task is take note of what news and
    information is given.

☐ Show the video:
  ▫ *What can they remember from the video?*

☐ Tell them that, for homework, they are going to create
  their own video letter to a friend or relative who lives
  in another country:
  ▫ They should explain what they do in their daily life.
  ▫ Using a mobile phone or other mobile device, they
    should film themselves at home and in other places
    they go to.
  ▫ They should talk about what they do in a normal day.

Post-production

The learners can upload their video to a video-sharing site
and send you a link, or send you a video file:
▫ You watch the video letters.
▫ You give feedback on content and presentation.

With their permission, you show the video letters to the class:
▫ They ask questions about what they see and hear in it.

The learners can imagine that the video letter is announcing
a major decision in their lives. It should not necessarily
be true, and could be very funny. Give the learners some
suggestions:
▫ They are going to give up their studies, to travel around
  the world.
▫ They are going to live with their partner, who their
  parents have never met.
▫ They are going to get married to their partner, who
  their parents cannot stand.
▫ They are going to give up a safe job, to do something
  they really love.

Filming a video comment

The learners record a comment on a viral video.

Pre-production

Select a short film on YouTube which has gone viral and
caused a lot of controversy.

For teachers who don't have time to source films themselves,
here is a link to a suitable viral video:
http://bit.ly/1ntJnGV

Action!

☐ Write *Viral short* on the board.

☐ Elicit or explain that it is a short film that becomes popular
  through the process of internet sharing, typically through
  video-sharing websites, social media and email:
  ▫ *Can the learners think of any examples of viral videos?*
  ▫ *Why do videos become viral?*

☐ Tell the learners they are going to watch a short film
  which went viral.

☐ Show the film.

☐ Pair the learners, to discuss:
  ▫ *What did they think of the video?*
  ▫ *Why do they think it went viral?*

☐ Tell them:
  ▫ They are going to write a positive or negative comment
    on the film they have just watched.
  ▫ They will then film each other commenting on the video.

☐ They should first write a short paragraph:
  ▫ Set a time limit of 10 minutes.
  ▫ Walk round, giving help as necessary.

☐ They practise reading the comment aloud several times:
  ▫ You help them with pronunciation.

☐ Pair the learners, to record each other commenting on
  the video, using a mobile phone or other mobile device.

☐ Hold a plenary session, discussing how they felt about
  the film and the comments they made about it.

Post-production

The learners send you a video file:
▫ You create a compilation of their 'video comments'
  videos.
▫ You show them, give feedback and discuss each comment.

For homework, the learners can choose a viral video which
has made a strong impact on them. They create a 'video
comment', expressing their opinion.

Recording a review

The learners practise film vocabulary,
and record their own film review.

Pre-production

Select a favourable movie review video.

For teachers who don't have time to source films themselves,
here is a link to a suitable video review:
http://bit.ly/11Bpbhk

Action!

☐ Pre-teach the film vocabulary opposite.

☐ Tell the learners they are going to watch a short movie
review:
  ▫ As they watch, their task is to listen for, and write
  down, any of the 'film vocabulary' that appears in
  the review.

☐ Show the film review twice.

☐ Pair the learners, to compare the words and phrases they
wrote down.

☐ Tell them you're going to show the film again:
  ▫ Their task, this time, is to tell you to pause every time
  one of the film vocabulary words or phrases is heard.

☐ Show the film and discuss the vocabulary:
  ▫ *Is the review favourable or unfavourable?*
  ▫ *Which words from the review support their opinion?*

☐ Tell the learners that they are going to make their own
one-minute film review videos:
  ▫ They think of a film which they have seen recently
  and liked.
  ▫ They plan what they are going to say in their review.

☐ Also tell them:
  ▫ They should try to use some of the film vocabulary
  and adjectives they heard in the review.
  ▫ They should make notes.

☐ You set a time limit of 10 minutes and walk round,
helping with language as necessary.

☐ Using their notes, the learners practise their reviews.

☐ They record their reviews on a webcam, mobile phone
or other mobile device.

☐ Ask the learners to upload the videos to YouTube. They
should watch the others' videos – to be able to comment
on them in the following lesson.

Set in	*Actor*	*Scene*
Directed by	*Director*	*Plot*
It stars	*Star*	*Story*
To play	*Character*	*Special effects*
To shoot	*Performance*	*Box office*

Post-production

You share the learners' videos with all the class, and
encourage them to comment on each other's video reviews.

Hands on!

The learners engage in the hands-on experience
of making a film.

Pre-production

Choose a website – Zimmer Twins is an excellent choice that
allows learners to create short animated film clips:
http://zimmertwinsatschool.com/

Set up a three-minute tutorial:
http://bit.ly/1lGNVI0.

This activity requires one computer per learner.

In the previous lesson, write the vocabulary opposite on the
board:
- Tell the learners to read the vocabulary, look up any words
  they don't know, and learn them for homework.
- Tell them they are going to need the vocabulary to create
  their own very short video, as it all appears on the website
  where they are going to make their films.

Action!

- ☐ Quickly revise the nouns and adjectives from the previous
  lesson.
- ☐ Show the learners the three-minute tutorial.
- ☐ With the learners at their computers, tell them to go to
  the address below. They will need to join, but they don't
  have to pay anything:
  http://zimmertwinsatschool.com/
- ☐ Their task is to write a funny, short dialogue.
- ☐ Tell them to click on the 'Create Movie' button and then
  the 'Make From Scratch' button.
- ☐ Tell them:
  - There are only three characters: the Zimmer twins
    (Eli and Eva) and the cat (called Thirteen).
  - They will create their film using these three characters,
    the actions and the speech bubbles.
- ☐ If they need any help, they can watch the tutorial again:
  - When they have finished, they watch their videos
    before they save them.
  - When they are happy with the videos, they click on
    the 'Save Movie' button.
- ☐ Ask them to send you a link to the videos.
- ☐ Showcase the videos, and get the learners to vote for the
  funniest.

Verbs			
agree	announce	call	celebrate
chase	crowd	surf	dance	disagree
drop	examine	faint	fall	find
fly	float	give	hide	hug	land
laugh	leave	lecture	levitate
meet	play	plot	plug	ears
read aloud	ride	rock	run	seek
sing	sit	sleep	sneak	stand
steal	strut	talk	tease	teleport
think	wake	walk	whisper	yell

Adjectives			
angry	bored	confused	dizzy
happy	impressed	relieved	scared
surprised	suspicious		

Post-production

The learners can create another movie at home:
- You give them 10 items of vocabulary they have studied
  recently.
- They should include this vocabulary in their dialogues.

They send you a link to their videos and you give them
feedback on their dialogues and their use of the vocabulary.

Animated grammar

Making a short animated movie,
using specific language.

Pre-production

Choose a website that allows the learners to create animated videos. Go Animate is an excellent choice:
http://goanimate.com/

Set up a three-minute tutorial:
http://bit.ly/1cNuso0

This activity requires one computer per learner.

Action!

☐ Tell the learners that they are going to create their own very short video – and practise a specific grammatical point at the same time.

☐ Show them the three-minute tutorial.

☐ With the learners at their computers, tell them to go to the address below. They will need to register, but they don't have to pay anything:
http://goanimate.com/

☐ Tell them which grammatical point you would like them to practise:
  ☐ Their task is to write a very short dialogue, using the target language.

☐ The learners create an animated video, using the dialogue:
  ☐ If they need any help, they can watch the tutorial again.
  ☐ If they want to add audio, they can use a microphone.

☐ When they have finished, they watch their videos before they save them.

☐ When they are happy with their videos, they click on the 'Save Movie' button.

☐ Ask them to send you a link to their videos.

☐ Showcase the videos, and get the learners to vote for the best/funniest/most original.

Post-production

Go Animate can be used for a lot more activities.

For learners:
  ☐ To create news bulletins.
  ☐ To create monologues of characters telling jokes or stories.
  ☐ To create soap operas, adding a new scene every week.

For teachers:
  ☐ To show scenes from real films or TV series, and get the learners to recreate the scene.
  ☐ To create short scenes, using the target language to present the language in context.

Visual poetry

The learners use their imagination
to create a visual poem.

Pre-production

Find a simple poem you think your learners will enjoy.

Action!

☐ Read out the poem:
  ☐ *What images spring to mind?*
  ☐ *How does the poem make the learners feel?*

☐ Give the learners the poem, and ask them to read it:
  ☐ You help them with any vocabulary or expressions they find difficult.

☐ Elicit or explain the meaning of the poem.

☐ Tell the learners they are going to create a 'visual poem' for homework.

☐ They have to find online images which they think represent your poem well:
  ☐ They import the images into a film-editing application or digital storytelling application.
  ☐ They read the poem aloud several times, and then add the audio to the video.

☐ In the following lesson, the learners watch each other's videos and comment on them.

Post-production

The learners can choose a poem *they* enjoy and create a visual poem to accompany it.

Alternatively, they can write *their own* poem and create a visual poem to accompany that.

This is a good follow-up activity to *My poem* on page 75.

Filming a dialogue

The learners memorise lines of a dialogue, perform and film the scene.

Pre-production

Select a film scene which has interesting dialogue you think your learners will enjoy. Make a transcript of the dialogue.

Teachers who don't have time to source films for themselves will find a link to a suitable film clip here: *http://bit.ly/1iqlGSq*

In the previous session, show the scene, give the learners the transcript and ask them to act it out:
- For homework, ask them to memorise their lines.

Action!

☐ Tell the learners they are going to perform and film their dialogues.

☐ Put them into threes. Two learners will perform the dialogue, while the third learner is the film director whose role is:
  - To make sure the actors know their lines by heart.
  - To set up the scene (choose the location, arrange furniture and any props, etc).
  - To tell the actors where to stand or sit.
  - To plan the shots.

☐ When the 'director' is happy that the learners know their lines and has set up the scene:
  - The two 'actors' perform their dialogue.
  - The director records it on a video camera or mobile device.

Post-production

The directors send you a video file. You watch the videos and give the learners feedback on performance and pronunciation.

As a further activity, the learners can create their own dialogues for given situations, such as:
- Announcing a life-changing event to a partner.
- Giving some bad news.
- Finishing a romantic relationship.
- Telling their boss they're leaving a job they hate.
- Confessing a dark secret to their romantic partner.

Filming a speech

The learners perform a speech, and film the scene.

Pre-production

Select a film scene which has a speech you think your learners will enjoy. Make a transcript of the speech.

Teachers who don't have time to source films for themselves will find a link to a suitable film clip here: *http://bit.ly/1fF8ab4*

In the previous session, show the scene, give the learners the transcript and help them with intonation and stress:
- For homework, the learners read the speech aloud several times.

Action!

☐ Pair the learners, to read out and record the speech they practised for homework.

☐ Before recording it, they practise the speech with their partner.

☐ One learner is the director whose role is:
  - To make sure the actor knows the speech well.
  - To set up the scene (choose the location, arrange furniture and any props, etc).
  - To tell the actor where to stand or sit.
  - To plan the shots.

☐ The director films the other learner performing the speech with a camera or mobile device.

☐ The learners then reverse roles.

Post-production

The learners send you the video file. You watch the videos and give them feedback on their presentation and pronunciation.

For homework, the learners can select a film scene which has a speech they like:
- They find the transcript, read the speech aloud several times and record themselves saying the speech.
- They send you the file and you give them feedback.

You can find an example of this activity here: *http://bit.ly/UB6DKT*

Filming an interview

Performing an interview between a journalist and an actor.

Pre-production

Find an interview between a journalist and an actor.

Teachers who don't have time to source films for themselves will find a link to a suitable interview here: *http://bit.ly/1vtadpj*

Action!

- ☐ Ask the learners what questions a journalist asks when interviewing an actor:
  - ☐ Elicit questions with the 'five Ws and an H' (*what, when, where, who, why* and *how*).

- ☐ Tell them they are going to watch an interview between a journalist and an actor. As they watch, their task is:
  - ☐ To check if the questions they mentioned are asked.
  - ☐ To note down any other questions.

- ☐ Show the interview, elicit the questions asked, and write them on the board.

- ☐ Divide the class into pairs:
  - ☐ One learner is a journalist.
  - ☐ One learner is one of their favourite actors, and tells their partner the name.

- ☐ They are going to hold an interview:
  - ☐ The *journalists* are going to interview their partner. They prepare questions, using the five Ws and an H.
  - ☐ The *actors* are going to be asked the questions. The actors should also prepare their own questions – as they will be changing roles after the interview, and will become the journalists.

- ☐ If you have access to the internet, or using the learners' mobile phones, ask them to find out some more information about their actor:
  - ☐ You set a time limit of 10 minutes.
  - ☐ You walk round, helping with language as necessary.

- ☐ The learners now interview each other, then you invite them to perform their interviews again:
  - ☐ This time, they record them on a mobile phone, tablet or video camera.

- ☐ Now repeat the interview procedure, with the learners exchanging roles.

- ☐ Show the videos in the next lesson, for learner comment.

Post-production

You can ask the learners to upload their videos to YouTube – and share them with all the class, encouraging them to comment on each other's interviews.

Filming a news report

Writing and recording a news report.

Pre-production

Write examples of *Who, What, Where, When, Why* and *How* questions, such as:

- ☐ *Who is it about?*
- ☐ *What happened?*
- ☐ *Where did it happen?*
- ☐ *When did it happen?*
- ☐ *Why did it happen?*
- ☐ *How did it happen?*

Action!

- ☐ Ask the learners:
  - ☐ *What information do they want to find out, when they read or watch a news item?*

- ☐ Elicit the question words *Who, What, Where, When, Why* and *How* – the five Ws and an H – and write them on the board.

- ☐ Tell the learners that the five Ws and an H are questions asked by journalists to provide the basic information about a news story.

- ☐ Dictate your example questions.

- ☐ Put the learners into threes, to imagine they are 'news teams':
  - ☐ They have 15 minutes to write the script of a short news story in which they answer the six questions.
  - ☐ They will have to choose a title for their news item.
  - ☐ They will then film themselves reporting the story.

- ☐ When the news teams have finished their script, two of the learners present the news item while the third learner is the film director whose role is:
  - ☐ To make sure the news presenters know the script by heart.
  - ☐ To set up the scene (choose the location, arrange the furniture and any props, etc).
  - ☐ To tell the news presenters where to stand or sit.
  - ☐ To plan the shots.

- ☐ When the 'director' is happy that the 'presenters' know their lines and has set up the scene, they present their news item and the director records it on a video camera or other mobile device.

Post-production

The director sends you a video file. You watch the film and give feedback on content, presentation and pronunciation.

In subsequent lessons, show the films to the class for the learners to comment. Ensure that they have addressed the questions and managed to answer all six.

This is an excellent follow-up activity to *Five Ws and an H* on page 43.

Filming an interrogation

The learners improvise and record
the police questioning of a witness.

Pre-production
Prepare some questions which the police might ask a witness
about a crime. See opposite.

Action!

☐ Ask the learners if they can remember any film scenes
in which the police question a witness:
- *What kind of questions do the police ask?*

☐ Elicit or explain some typical questions the police ask
witnesses:
- Tell the learners they are going to perform and film a
police officer questioning a witness.

☐ Put the learners into threes, to choose one of the following
dramatic situations:
- A murder
- A political assassination
- A bank robbery
- A fight
- An accident

☐ The first student is a witness who was present at the
dramatic event:
- They visualise the event in as much detail as possible.
- They prepare to be interviewed by a police officer.

☐ The second student is a suspicious police officer who is
going to question the witness:
- They have to prepare questions to ask the witness.
- If they don't understand any of the witness's answers,
they should ask further questions.

☐ The third learner is the film director whose role is to:
- Set up the scene (choose the location, arrange furniture
and any props, etc).
- Tell the actors where to stand or sit.
- Plan the shots.

☐ When the director has set up the scene:
- The witness and the police officer perform their
improvised dialogue.
- The third learner records it on a video camera
or mobile device.

> ☐ *Did you see what he/she was wearing?*
>
> ☐ *Can you describe him/her for me?*
>
> ☐ *Was he/she wearing a mask?*
>
> ☐ *Did he/she have a weapon?*
>
> ☐ *Was the gun loaded?*
>
> ☐ *Did you hear a shot?*
>
> ☐ *What kind of car was the thief/robber/murderer driving?*
>
> ☐ *Would you recognise the thief/robber/murderer if you saw him/her again?*

Post-production
The directors send you a video file. You watch the videos
and give the learners feedback on performance and
pronunciation.

This is an excellent follow-up activity to *Eyewitness account*
on page 52.

Filming a title sequence

Creating the opening titles for an invented film.

Pre-production

Select an interesting opening title sequence. Hundreds of beautiful examples can be found at Art of the Title:
http://www.artofthetitle.com/

Action!

☐ Write *Opening title* sequence on the board:
- ☐ Elicit or explain that this is the method by which films present their title, cast members, director and key members of the production team at the beginning or end of a film.
- ☐ Elicit or explain the vocabulary of *cast*, *crew* and *production team* – if necessary.

☐ Tell the learners they are going to watch the opening title sequence of a film.

☐ Their task is to identify:
- ☐ The title
- ☐ The film studio
- ☐ The main actors
- ☐ The director
- ☐ Other key members of the production team

☐ Show the title sequence.

☐ Tell the learners to imagine that a biopic film is going to be made about *their* life:
- ☐ Their task is to create a title sequence for the film.

☐ They should note down the title, cast members, director and key members of the production team.

☐ They create the opening titles, using Windows Movie Maker or Apple iMovie.

Post-production

The learners upload their videos to YouTube and send you a link:
- ☐ You watch the videos.
- ☐ You give the learners feedback.

You showcase the videos, and you all vote on the best opening title sequence.

This is an excellent follow-up to *Opening titles* on page 36.

Making a 'how to' video

The learners create an instructional video, using a mobile device.

Pre-production

Select a video which you think your learners will enjoy, which shows how to do something.

Two excellent websites which provide short instructional 'how to' videos are:
Howcast – *http://www.howcast.com/*
Videojug – *http://www.videojug.com/*

For teachers who don't have time to source films themselves, here is a link to a suitable 'how to' video:
http://bit.ly/1tVEg4A

Action!

☐ Tell the learners they are going to watch a video entitled 'How to …':
- ☐ *What instructions do they think they will see and hear?*

☐ As they watch the video, their task will be to check their predictions.

☐ Show the video.

☐ Tell the learners they are now going to create their own 'how to' videos, using a mobile phone or other mobile device:
- ☐ They decide what activity they would like to describe.
- ☐ They then write a short script.

☐ They read their script aloud several times, and then video each other explaining how to do the activity.

☐ Each learner shows their video on their mobile device to another learner.

☐ Hold a plenary session, based on the learners' videos.

Post-production

After the lesson, the learners send you a video file:
- ☐ You watch their videos.
- ☐ You give them feedback.

For homework, they can choose 'how to' videos which they find interesting:
- ☐ They watch them several times.
- ☐ They then film themselves giving the same instructions.

This is an excellent follow-up activity to *'How to' films* on page 71.

Making a branded short

Preparing and giving a short presentation
on a short film for a brand.

Pre-production

Select a branded short (a short film which has been created
for a company or product).

Teachers who don't have time to source films for themselves
will find a link to a suitable short film here:
http://bit.ly/1k9ypUE

Action!

☐ Elicit or explain that a branded short is a short film
   created for a company or product.

☐ Show your branded short:
   ▫ *What company or product is being advertised?*
   ▫ *How does the film support this brand?*

☐ Ask the learners to imagine that they are advertising
   executives who want to make a short film for a company
   or product.

☐ Divide the class into groups of three:
   ▫ Each group chooses the company or product they want
     to advertise.

☐ Tell the groups their task is:
   ▫ To decide how they would make their short.
   ▫ To break the film into important points.
   ▫ To write very brief notes on the action, dialogue,
     camera shots and angles, and sound effects and music.

☐ Tell them they are going to perform and film their
   presentation.

☐ Two learners perform the presentation, while the third
   learner is the film director whose role is:
   ▫ To make sure the executives know their lines by heart.
   ▫ To set up the scene (choose the location, arrange the
     furniture and any props, etc).
   ▫ To tell the executives where to stand or sit.
   ▫ To plan the shots.

☐ When the 'director' is happy that the others know their
   lines and has set up the scene:
   ▫ The two 'executives' perform their dialogue.
   ▫ The director records it on a mobile phone or other
     mobile device.

Post-production

The director sends you a video file. You watch the video
files and give the learners feedback on performance and
pronunciation.

This is an excellent follow-up to *Branded shorts* on page 68.

Making a response video

Thinking critically about viral short films and videos
commissioned by companies.

Pre-production

Select a short film commissioned by a large company, which
has gone viral and provoked a response video by another
film-maker.

For teachers who don't have time to source films themselves,
here is a link to a suitable short film:
http://bit.ly/1p07ywu

Action!

☐ Tell the learners they are going to watch a short film
   which was commissioned by a big company:
   ▫ Introduce the theme of the film.
   ▫ Pre-teach any necessary vocabulary.
   ▫ Dictate some discussion questions.
   ▫ Ask the learners to discuss them in pairs.

☐ Tell the class that after watching the film, they are going
   to imagine they are film-makers who want to parody or
   criticise the original film.

☐ Show the film.

☐ Give the name of the company which has commissioned
   the film:
   ▫ *Do they know anything about it?*

☐ If not, give them some information about it, then divide
   the class into small groups:
   ▫ *As film-makers, how could they make a response film
     which criticises or parodies the original film?*

☐ They write the script.

☐ They read their script aloud several times:
   ▫ They video themselves criticising or parodying the film.
   ▫ You set a time limit of 20 minutes.

☐ Each group presents their video on a mobile phone or
   other mobile device to another group.

☐ Hold a plenary session, based on the learners' proposals.

Post-production

After the lesson, the learners send you a video file. You watch
their videos and give them feedback.

For homework, they can find viral videos which have had
a strong impact on them. They write a script, and create
a response video.

This is an excellent follow-up to *Response films* on page 69.

Making a remake

The learners create and film a plan to remake a film.

Pre-production

Think of examples of remakes which your learners are likely to know. Make sufficient copies of a worksheet like the one opposite.

Action!

☐ Write *Remake* on the board:
  ☐ Elicit or explain that it is a new version of an old film.
  ☐ Give *your* examples of remakes.

☐ Ask the learners for examples of remakes *they* have seen.

☐ Divide the class into groups of three, and distribute the worksheet:
  ☐ The groups' task is to imagine they are film producers and film directors who want to make a remake of a well-known film.

☐ In their groups, they discuss their ideas, and complete the worksheet.

☐ Once they have finished, tell them they are going to do the following:
  ☐ They will write a script to present their plan.
  ☐ They will film themselves presenting their plan to a group of investors.

☐ Two 'producers' will perform the script, while the other learner is the director of the film whose role is:
  ☐ To make sure the producers know the script by heart.
  ☐ To set up the scene (choose the location, arrange the furniture and any props, etc).
  ☐ To tell the producers where to stand or sit.
  ☐ To plan the shots.

☐ When the 'director' has set up the scene and is happy that the other two learners know their lines:
  ☐ The two producers perform their dialogue.
  ☐ The director records it on a video camera or other mobile device.

Post-production

The director sends you a video file:
  ☐ You watch the videos.
  ☐ You give the learners feedback on their scripts and presentation.

For homework, the learners can write a composition in which they compare a film and its remake.

Making a remake
Original title
New title
New genre
Setting
Cast
Soundtrack

Presenting a movie pitch

Writing and filming a film sales pitch.

Pre-production

Find a video which gives advice on how to make a
movie pitch.

Teachers who don't have time to source films for themselves
will find a link to a suitable film clip here:
http://bit.ly/1CoZQIf

Action!

☐ Write *Pitch* on the board.

☐ Explain that a movie pitch is a concise presentation of
an idea for a film, generally made by a scriptwriter or
director to a producer or studio executive – in the hope of
attracting money to finance the film:
  ◻ *What should a person making a movie pitch do?*
  ◻ *What shouldn't they do?*

☐ Show a video which gives advice on how to make a movie
pitch, and ask the learners to try to remember the advice:
  ◻ They compare *their* advice with the advice given in the
  video.

☐ Pair the learners:
  ◻ They are scriptwriters and directors who want to
  convince a studio to make their film.
  ◻ Their task is to write a pitch which sells their film
  to studio executives.

☐ Tell them that the studio will probably want the
information below:
  ◻ *What story does the film tell?*
  ◻ *Who are the main characters?*
  ◻ *How might the film be cast?*
  ◻ *How much will it cost to make?*
  ◻ *How will they market it?*
  ◻ *What films does it resemble?*

☐ The learners write their pitch.

☐ They will have three minutes to deliver it, and they should
make sure they include:
  ◻ All the information.
  ◻ Enough persuasive language to convince the studio
  to make their film.

☐ Set a time limit of 10 minutes and walk round, providing
help with language as necessary.

☐ When the learners are ready, put the pairs together:
  ◻ One pair are *scriptwriter* and *director*, who have to
  persuade the other pair to make their film.
  ◻ The other pair are two *studio executives*.

☐ Remind them that the pitch should last no longer than
three minutes:
  ◻ Tell the scriptwriters and directors that they have to
  sell their film with great enthusiasm and convince the
  studio executives that it's going to be the blockbuster
  of the year.
  ◻ Tell the studio executives to make sure they get all the
  information they need.

☐ The learners act out their scene.

☐ You then reverse the roles and repeat the movie pitches.

☐ Invite volunteer pairs to act out their pitches for the rest
of the class.

☐ Finally, ask the learners to film each other's pitches on
a mobile phone or other mobile device.

Post-production

The learners send you their videos:
  ◻ You watch them.
  ◻ You give the learners feedback on their presentation and
  pronunciation.

Show the videos in the following lesson, for the learners to
vote on the best/funniest/most original sales pitch.

The learners can also create a pitch for a music video, advert
or viral video.

Film in Action has so far examined the role of film in society, education and language learning. It has also suggested many ways of engaging your learners by focusing on film to teach language skills, helping them to interpret and analyse film and encouraging them to create their own films.

We can now look at ways for you to fully incorporate film into the wider environment of the school and the syllabus.

In order to integrate film successfully into both school and syllabus, it is essential that film is not treated as an optional extra or an add-on subject. We need, also, to adopt clear operating principles, such as the 'three Cs' approach we looked at in Part A:

- **Cultural access** Learners need to have the opportunity to choose from a wide range of films, in order to get a better understanding of their own culture and those of others.
- **Critical understanding** Learners should be able to analyse critically a film's intentions, techniques and qualities.
- **Creative activity** Learners must finally be allowed the opportunity to create their own moving image texts.

The four projects we shall be presenting in Part C are all designed around those three broad, overlapping and dynamic themes.

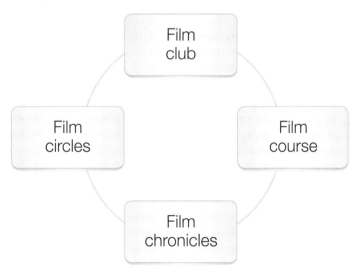

Film club

The easiest way to integrate film into the life of a school is by starting a film club. Setting up a film club is fun, rewarding, supports informal learning and requires no special skills.

There are many benefits to film clubs, which give young people the opportunity to watch, discuss and review a diverse range of films:

- Learners who participate in extracurricular activities tend to be more successful in their school, professional and personal lives.
- Film clubs help promote young people's linguistic, intellectual, social and cultural development. Advantages for members include developing a wide range of skills, increasing enjoyment of school and integrating isolated pupils.
- Discussing and reviewing films helps learners develop skills in critical analysis, literacy and communication.
- Screening regularly a broad variety of films increases learners' cultural and intercultural awareness.

Getting started

The first step is to make an outline of the club, which you can present to school management. Here are some of the things you might like to include in your outline:

- **Mission statement** Express what your club's goals are. *What do you want to achieve?*
- **Structure** Explain briefly how your club will be run. *Who is going to be the chairperson, treasurer, publicity officer, projectionist, etc? Are the members going to be assigned roles and responsibilities?*
- **Budget** Explore if your school has already got the equipment you need (PC, data projector, screen, blinds, DVDs, etc). *Do you need to purchase or hire them? Is membership free, or are you going to charge a fee?*

Choosing the room

Every film club needs a 'cinema'. A good venue should have the following:

- A means of projecting film (a PC, data projector and screen are enough).
- An adequate sound system.
- Blinds, or a means of blacking-out. If you can't black out the room, you will need a more powerful projector.
- Enough comfortable seats – or bean bags for younger members.

Checking the legal implications

It may be necessary to obtain licences, prior to opening the doors of your film club:

- *Does your venue have a public screening licence?*
- *Does the school's public liability insurance cover a film club?*
- *Are there any restrictions under your school's fire and building regulations?*

Selecting the films

It is important to try to create a balance:

- Supplement commercial mainstream films with more challenging and adventurous choices, such as documentaries, classic, black and white and arthouse films.
- Make your first screening attention-grabbing and memorable, by showing a film you are convinced your members will love.
- Once your club is successfully up and running, gradually introduce a broader range of films to give your members a fuller cultural experience.

Spreading the word

Every film club needs members and, if your films are not publicised, it is unlikely many people will come to see them:

- Create attractive and informative posters, and place them in classrooms and throughout the school.
- Create a film club blog, where the learners can easily find the programme of forthcoming films.
- Ask your members to write reviews of the films they see, and to upload them to the club blog.
- Ask your members to publicise the films among their friends.
- Announce the films in your own classes, and ask other teachers to mention the film club in their classes.

Looking towards the future

When your club is really off the ground, allow it to evolve and change according to the demands of the members:

- Let your club members help shape how the club is run.
- Allow your programme to be a balance between what *you* would like to show, and what *your members* want to see.

Taking care of the present

Here are some tips for setting off on the right foot, and for maintaining the right direction:

- Try to replicate the ambience and atmosphere of a cinema by pulling the blinds down or covering the windows, and by turning off the lights. The layout of the room is vital for a club to be a success.
- Create a fun atmosphere, with popcorn and other snacks. They are a great way to fundraise – have members or parents make cakes and provide drinks to sell every week in your film club.
- Ensure your screenings are regular, to achieve consistent attendance. Clubs run most efficiently if held every week.
- Try to choose the same space each week to run your club.
- Choose your screening day and time carefully, to ensure that as many learners as possible can come.
- Allow enough time to introduce the film and be able to hold a post-screening discussion.
- Encourage regular attendance and dedicated membership. When they see the same members every week, the learners start to feel both a sense of ownership over their club and feel safe to express themselves during discussion activities.

- Ask for volunteers to help run the club. Assigning roles and responsibilities to your members (DVD responsibility, moving tables/chairs, setting up the equipment, introducing the film, promotion) also gives them a sense of ownership over the film club.
- Present the idea of exclusivity, by the use of membership cards and badges.
- Have clear club rules, and make sure the members know them and what is expected of them as members.
- Advertise forthcoming films on a noticeboard, creating interest in the club.
- Make and print cinema tickets for each film and distribute them to members. Have a member who is responsible for checking and tearing tickets as your members enter the 'cinema'.
- Hold screenings for friends and families. Invite the members to watch a film with their friends and families.

Film course

A highly effective way to integrate film into the school and syllabus is to set up an *English through Film* course, aimed at learners who want to improve and practise their language through the medium of film and their passion for cinema. Film can be used to generate activities in speaking, listening, reading and writing.

Course definition
The fundamental difference between a film club and a film course is this:
- In a film club, the learners gather for an extra-curricular activity to enjoy a cinematic experience – they watch a whole feature film in one sitting; they then discuss the film they have just seen.
- In a film course, the learners take a series of classes in which they improve their English – through the study, analysis and discussion of film.

Course objectives
As with any course, for it to succeed it is essential to have clear pedagogical goals. These may include:
- To develop the learners' spoken and written accuracy and range of vocabulary around specified topic areas related to the films they watch.
- To develop the learners' range of vocabulary related to film, film genres and film analysis.
- To develop fluency in interactive communication, through guided and freer discussion of issues related to topic areas presented in the films.
- To develop the learners' ability to analyse and interpret moving image texts.
- To develop the learners' critical thinking skills.
- To develop the learners' intercultural communicative competence through viewing a wide range of films.

- To provide the learners with an inside view of the English-speaking world through viewing of films.
- To provide critical feedback on presentations and reviews, and to allow the learners to hone the skills and language needed to deliver information and opinion about a film effectively in both oral and written form.

Course selection
It is important to try to show a broad range of films – classic, contemporary, blockbuster, little-known, black and white, 3D, European, non-European – to take your learners on diverse film journeys and to expose them to different cultural perspectives:
- At the beginning of the course, give the learners a list of all the films you have chosen so that they can find the films.
- In the first week of the course, in addition to the films that you choose, each learner should select one of their favourite films which the group will watch during the course.
- Throughout the course, programme the films in the following way: one week, the learners watch a film *you* have selected; the next week, they watch a film which *another learner* has selected.

Course activities
From my experience, this type of course is very popular and highly motivating for learners, who are able to develop all four skills through communicative activities based on film.

However, the problem I have encountered in doing a number of these courses is that they are very time-consuming:
- If teachers prepare their own worksheets for each film, this involves watching the film several times.
- It also possibly involves transcribing the dialogue.

The solution to this problem is threefold:
- You can use generic activities which require little or no preparation by the teacher, such as those found in Part B of *Film in Action*.
- Your learners can select films they want the rest of the group to watch, and prepare their own brief film guide and discussion questions about the film.
- You can use existing film guides which have been created by other teachers or institutions.

Film guides
Every week, give the learners one of the film guides:
- For homework, they have to first read the guide and then watch the film.
- In the next class, they discuss different aspects of the film.
- They engage in discussions and debates, after watching clips of the film.

They can also do a range of communicative activities, related to a variety of short films and clips from films.

On page 102 are three sites which provide free and pedagogically-sound film guides.

ESL Notes (*http://www.eslnotes.com/*) is an excellent resource site created by an American ESL teacher, Raymond Weschler, which provides over 200 detailed film guides. Each individual guide is a detailed synopsis of a popular classic or contemporary film that consists of the following:

- A summary of the plot.
- A description of the main characters.
- An extensive glossary of vocabulary and expressions, and various cultural references.
- Discussion questions.

Film Education (*http://www.filmeducation.org/*) is part of the British Film Institute, producing engaging film guides for a wide range of films for primary and secondary school children. Although they are not specifically designed for language teaching, they include the following:

- Interesting pre-watching and post-watching discussion activities.
- Tasks which focus on developing visual literacy and intercultural communicative competence, which work very well with language learners.

Film Club (*http://www.filmclub.org/*) is a UK charity, which gives children and young people the opportunity to watch, discuss and review films. They supply hundreds of pedagogically interesting free film guides. Each individual guide does the following:

- Answer the questions *What's it about?* and *Who made it?*
- Give the learners background information and discussion questions.

Learner presentations

During the course, each learner has to choose one of their favourite films and then give a presentation of it to the rest of the group. They should also prepare a brief guide for the film, which they give to the rest of the group. The guide should include the following questions:

- *What's it about?* Synopsis of the film. The learners describe what happens in the film – but not too much!
- *Who made it?* Information about the director and their other films.
- *What do you think?* Questions about the film for the learners to consider:
  - *Which scene do you remember the most?*
  - *How memorable was the sound in the film?*
  - *What's the best part of the film – sound or pictures?*
  - *What do you think will happen to …?*
  - *Did you like the ending? What alternative endings can you imagine?*
  - *What surprised you about the film?*
  - *How would you describe the message of the film?*
  - *Did this film change your view of …?*
  - *Imagine the plot of the film transferred to your country or school. What would stay the same, and what would be different?*

In the session before their film is watched by the rest of the group, each learner has to give a brief presentation (maximum 15 minutes) where they answer these questions:

- *Why did I choose this film?*
- *What's the film about?*
- *Who made the film?*
- *What did I like about the film?*
- *What to look out for in the film?*

The learners give the teacher and the rest of the group the film guide they have prepared:

- The group watch the film at home.
- In the next session, they discuss the *What do you think?* questions.

Learner reviews

The learners should write a review of each of the films they view. You could give them a template to help structure it:

Writing a film review

Paragraph 1: Overall impression

- Give your general reaction to the film.
- Give the following information:
  - Title
  - Director
  - Year of release
  - Genre
  - Main actors

Paragraph 2: Plot summary

- Give a brief synopsis, but don't explain everything.
- Identify the main premise of the film.
- Is it convincing?

Paragraph 3: Acting

- How did the actors portray the key roles?

Paragraph 4: Film techniques

- Describe and assess the cinematography (camera angles, lighting, editing, etc).
- Describe and assess the soundtrack, special effects, costume design, etc.

Paragraph 5: Theme

- Identify the message of the film.
- Is the message conveyed effectively?

Paragraph 6: Conclusion

- Give your opinion of the film.
- Would you recommend the reader sees or avoids it?

Film course blog

Finally, you might like to set up a group blog, where the learners can share and comment on the reviews.

In my experience, I have found that they enjoy using the following blogging tools – as they are practical, user-friendly and intuitive:

- Wordpress – *https://wordpress.com/*
- Blogger – *https://blogger.com*

Film chronicles

We will now look at three film-making projects – chronicles – which can be easily integrated into the syllabus, and designed in such a way that much of the work can be done outside of school time or set as homework.

Your school or your learners probably already have the equipment you need, and they don't need a great deal of technical experience or support from you, their teacher.

The learners start with what is the easiest chronicle:
- They first make a film promoting their school.
- They then move out of the school to their homes, where they create a film about their family.
- Finally, they make a film about their local community.

See pages 104–105 for more details on each project.

The school film chronicle is done in groups, the family film is done individually, and the community film in pairs. All of the film projects take the learners out of the classroom:
- They help to *bridge the gap* between the curriculum and the world outside the classroom.
- They may also help to *build bridges* between the learners and their schools, families and wider communities.

These chronicles aim to develop the learners' abilities in the following areas:
- Reading and writing skills
- Speaking skills
- Paralinguistic skills
- Presentation skills
- Research skills
- Visualisation skills
- Problem-solving skills
- Critical thinking skills
- Planning and coordinating skills
- Creativity
- Self-confidence

By combining language learning with developing other skills, project-based learning – in this case a film chronicle – allows

the learners to connect the language of the classroom with the outside world and their own personal interests.

The major decisions about creating the films should be left to the learners, either individually or in their pairs or groups:
- They explore and develop an original idea.
- They prepare their own scripts.
- They rehearse and perform their scripts.
- They direct and edit their films.

However, you – the teacher – also play a number of roles:
- Helping your learners write their scripts, and making sure these are understandable.
- Ensuring their subtitles and captions are understandable.
- Advising them on their pronunciation, including the use of stress and intonation, when they are rehearsing their scripts.
- Advising them on paralinguistic features, such as body language, gestures and facial expressions.
- Giving feedback on their language errors.
- Evaluating their performance in the creative process of making a film, and their final 'products' – their films!

Making films manageable!

Digital film-making has not only made the process of creating a film much cheaper than ever before, but it has also made the process incredibly easier and less time-consuming. Nowadays, anyone with a digital camera or even a mobile device can be a film-maker.

The secret is keeping it simple:
- Use a basic video camera which is straightforward for the learners to operate. Your school will probably already have a suitable basic camera.
- Use a mobile phone camera or still camera that records movies, if your school hasn't got suitable cameras.
- Try to avoid using bulky cameras, which are difficult for the learners to use.
- Use basic film-editing software which comes with most computers. It isn't necessary to purchase professional editing software.
- Make films *without* a computer, using 'in-camera editing': you plan the shots carefully, then shoot them in the right order.
- Start by keeping your films short and simple. Making films just a few minutes long will already involve a lot of time-consuming work – and it may be all you need.
- Start with very tight film-making criteria and limit choice – to help your learners focus on what they have to do.
- As they get more proficient, you can give looser criteria to allow them greater creativity.

My school

The learners create a two-minute film to chronicle the history of their school. There are three main advantages to this project:

- Firstly, the logistics are relatively easy, as all the locations are within the school grounds.
- Secondly, as the learners are familiar with the school they may find it easier to research, plan and coordinate the project.
- Thirdly, the film can be used as a promotional tool for the school at, for example, school open days or parents' evenings.

If you have enough cameras, divide your class into teams of five members, and assign the learners their roles:

- Director
- Camera operator
- Sound technician
- Scriptwriter
- Presenter

Equipment needed

- At least one basic digital video camera.
- A computer with basic video-editing software.
- A data projector to show the film.

Learning goals – linguistic

- To use specific vocabulary related to the school and studying in an authentic setting.
- To use vocabulary and expressions related to film production.
- To improve presentation skills.
- To write and edit a script.
- To rehearse and memorise a script.

Learning goals – digital and visual literacy

- Basic handling of a film camera.
- Transfering film footage to a computer.
- Editing the film footage.
- Uploading and sharing the film online.

My family

In this chronicle, the learners make a two-minute film about their family. The main ideas behind this project are to create awareness of learners' families and to chronicle their stories, and – as the project is deeply personal – for the learners to engage meaningfully with language.

They research their own families, and then decide how to tell their families' stories. As the project criteria are quite loose, the learners can be creative in the way they tell these stories:

- Some will interview parents, siblings, grandparents and other relatives.
- Some will use photos and video footage to tell their stories.
- Others will re-create historical family events.

Equipment needed

- A basic digital video camera or stills camera/mobile phone with video function.
- A computer with basic video-editing software.

Learning goals – linguistic

- To use specific vocabulary related to family.
- To use past tenses.
- To write and edit a script or narrative.
- To rehearse and memorise a script.
- To translate a transcription into English.

Learning goals – digital and visual literacy

- Basic handling of a film camera.
- Transfering film footage to a computer.
- Editing the film footage.
- Adding subtitles to a film.
- Adding still images of family members to the film.
- Uploading and sharing the film online.

My community

In this chronicle, the learners work in pairs to create a five-minute film documentary about an artist who lives in their community. The principal idea is to create meaningful engagement with language through engagement with the learners' local community.

Making a documentary in the local community is a more ambitious and time-consuming project. However, if the activity is relevant and meaningful for the learners, the preparation and shooting of such a documentary is:

- linguistically valuable;
- deeply engaging;
- highly motivating;
- creative.

Films shot in the local community can contribute to the local community, as well as encourage cultural understanding.

As the project criteria are loose, the learners are given opportunities to explore their own interests and creativity:

- Some learners will interview DJs and graffiti artists.
- Others will choose buskers and street artists.

Equipment needed

- A basic digital video camera or stills camera/mobile phone with video function.
- A computer with basic video-editing software.

Learning goals – linguistic

- To use specific vocabulary related to art and artists.
- To write 'Wh' questions.
- To write and edit a script.
- To rehearse and memorise a script.
- To translate a transcription into English.

Learning goals – digital and visual literacy

- Basic handling of a film camera.
- Transfering film footage to a computer.
- Editing the film footage.
- Adding subtitles to a film.
- Adding music to the film.
- Uploading and sharing the film online.

Film circles

A film circle is a scaffolded, collaborative, highly communicative, roleplaying, task-based project. It promotes learner autonomy and makes learners more responsible for their own learning.

It can be used with any feature-length film. That said:
- It is important to make the learners part of the process of film selection.
- It is important to offer them the opportunity to choose from a broad range of films.

The first time you do this activity, it is very important to give the instructions very carefully:
- You must ensure the learners understand exactly what they have to do in their roles.
- The next time you do the activity, each learner will be assigned a different role.

The five roles are these:

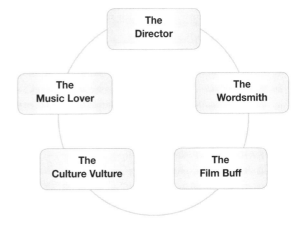

- *The Director* leads the group discussion and also asks questions to increase comprehension.
- *The Wordsmith* is responsible for finding the meaning and pronunciation of difficult words.
- *The Film Buff* is responsible for selecting three interesting scenes in the film and helping the other members to analyse them.
- *The Culture Vulture* is responsible for finding information about the cultural setting of the film.
- *The Music Lover* is responsible for finding out about the songs from the film.

A film circle is divided into two parts: *Critical understanding* and *Creative expression*. Learners are put into groups of five, and each learner is assigned a role and has to carry out tasks related to that role:
- In the *Critical understanding* stage, they are invited to understand and appreciate the multi-faceted nature of film.
- In the *Creative expression* stage, they produce their own moving image texts in response to the film they watched.

The *Critical understanding* stage

Aim
The learners research a film and find information relevant to their specific task. They then watch the film, do their tasks and report back to their group in the next session.

Each member of each group engages in cooperative learning, contributes to the discussion, and practises speaking.

Pre-production
Select a film from a wide range of films which you think your learners will enjoy, but which will also challenge them:
- Prepare role worksheets like those below. (Our sample worksheet is for a film with soundtrack songs.)
- Make enough copies for your learners.

Action!
Divide the class into groups of five, and assign each learner one of the following roles: *The Director*, *The Wordsmith*, *The Film Buff*, *The Culture Vulture* and *The Music Lover*:
- Tell them that they have to research the film you chose, to find information relevant to their specific task.

Give each learner a worksheet – see below – for their role:
- Tell them the film you want them to watch at home, or you view the film in class.

At home, the learners research the information relevant to their role and report back to their group in the next session:
- Tell them that it is very important that everyone performs their task, otherwise the reporting-back session won't work well and they will have let down the other members of their group.

In the following session, the director leads the discussion and asks questions to improve comprehension:
- Each member reports back on what they found out.

Hold a plenary session on what they have all gained from the project so far.

Post-production
For homework, the learners can write a composition on what they learnt about the film.

The Director

- Watch the film, and prepare five questions about it.
- Prepare questions to start the film circle discussion.
- Direct the discussion.
- Make sure that everyone in the film circle has a chance to speak.

The discussion works best when you write your own questions, but here are five questions which may be useful:

1 *Why do you think the director had* _____ *happen in the film?*

2 *How is* _____ *alike/different from* _____ ?

3 *If you had been* _____ *, how would you have* _____ ?

4 *How did you feel about* _____ ?

5 *What do you think caused* _____ ?

The Wordsmith

- Watch the film.
- Look for words or expressions that are new or difficult to understand, that are used frequently, or that are important in the story the film tells.

- Choose five words or expressions you think are important for this film.
- Write down the sentences in which the words or expressions appear.
- Find out the meanings of the words and expressions, and how to pronounce them.

- Explain the meanings and pronunciation of the words and expressions to the other members of the group.
- Tell the group why the words and expressions are important to the meaning of the film.

Minute and second	Word or expression	Sentence from film	Definition	Pronunciation

The Film Buff

- Watch the film, and choose three scenes you think are particularly important.
- Make notes about why the scenes are important to the plot.
- Explain to the group your reasons for selecting the scenes, and why they are important.
- Ask the group some questions about each scene.

Scene 1
Minute and second:

Why did you choose this scene?

What do you want the other members of the group to look at in this scene?

Scene 2
Minute and second:

Why did you choose this scene?

What do you want the other members of the group to look at in this scene?

Scene 3
Minute and second:

Why did you choose this scene?

What do you want the other members of the group to look at in this scene?

The Culture Vulture

- Watch the film, and look for both similarities and differences between your culture and the culture shown in the film.
- Make notes about three scenes that show these cultural similarities and differences.
- Explain to the group the scenes and cultural points you chose.
- Ask the group some questions about each scene and cultural point.

Discussion works best when you write your own questions, but here are five questions which may be useful:

- *What kind of culture is shown in the scene?*
- *How is the culture shown in the scene similar to that of your country?*
- *How is the culture shown in the scene different to that of your country?*
- *Is the theme of the scene an important one in your culture?*
- *Do people in your country think about this theme in the same way?*

The Music Lover

- Watch the film, paying attention to the soundtrack.
- Choose three songs which you think are important in the film.
- Find the lyrics to the songs and look up any words and expressions you don't understand.
- Explain to the group why you selected the songs and why they are important in the film.
- Give the lyrics of one of the songs to the other members of the group and explain their meaning.

Song 1
Minute and second:

Why did you choose this song?

What emotions were shown in the film when this song was heard?

Song 2
Minute and second:

Why did you choose this song?

What emotions were shown in the film when this song was heard?

Song 3
Minute and second:

Why did you choose this song?

What emotions were shown in the film when this song was heard?

Acknowledgement

This stage of *Film circles* is freely adapted from an activity in Lisa Fink's *Literature Circle* lesson plan:
http://www.readwritethink.org/classroom-resources/lesson-plans/literature-circles-getting-started-19.html#overview;
and an activity from the OUP *Bookworms* series.

The *Creative activity* stage

After the learners have explored and discussed the multiple facets of the film in the *Critical understanding* stage:

- They can now be given the opportunity to be creative and produce their own moving text inspired by the film they have watched.
- They can follow the following seven-step process, which can be used in any film-making project in the classroom.

Step 1 – Preparing

Each learner remains in the same role: *The Director, The Wordsmith, The Film Buff, The Culture Vulture* and *The Music Lover*. However, their tasks are now different:

- Tell them that they are going to create their own film in response to the film they have watched, by adapting a scene to their own cultural setting.
- Tell them that they have to prepare, by doing the tasks relevant to their specific role.

Give each learner their pre-production tasks:

- *The Director* is the person who takes overall responsibility for the project and helps the other members of the group with any problems they might have in performing their tasks. The director is also the person who decides on locations, helps the other members rehearse and memorise the script, prepares the camera, microphone and tripod, and rehearses the recording.
- *The Wordsmith* is responsible for writing the script.
- *The Film Buff* is responsible for creating the storyboard, selecting the type of shots to be used and filming the scene.
- *The Culture Vulture* is responsible for adapting the cultural setting of the film.
- *The Music Lover* is the person who decides on the music used and adds it to the film.

Each learner performs their pre-production tasks, which may take place over a number of sessions.

Step 2 – Rehearsing

When the directors are happy that all the members of the group have performed their pre-production tasks, they decide which members are going to perform the dialogue, and then help them rehearse and memorise the script. Rehearsal is very important:

- As the learners repeat the language, they will become more fluent.
- As the learners practise the script, they may realise that some elements need to be modified or changed.

When the directors are sure the actors know their lines by heart, their role is to do the following:

- Set up the scene (choose the location, arrange furniture and any props, etc).
- Tell the actors where to stand or sit.
- Plan the shots together with the film buff.
- Rehearse the recording with all the members of the group.

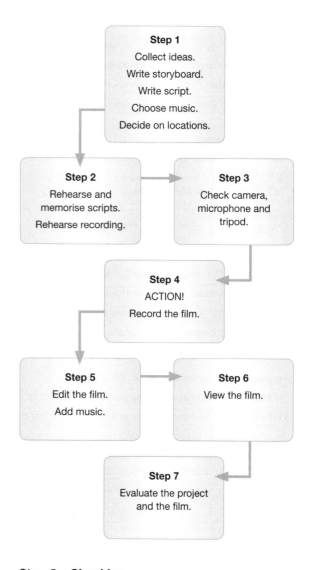

Step 1
Collect ideas.
Write storyboard.
Write script.
Choose music.
Decide on locations.

Step 2
Rehearse and memorise scripts.
Rehearse recording.

Step 3
Check camera, microphone and tripod.

Step 4
ACTION!
Record the film.

Step 5
Edit the film.
Add music.

Step 6
View the film.

Step 7
Evaluate the project and the film.

Step 3 – Checking

The director and the film buff make sure that all the equipment is working; they check the camera, microphone and tripod.

Step 4 – Recording

The actors perform their dialogue, and the film buff records it on a video camera or mobile device while the director supervises the whole process.

Step 5 – Editing

The learners edit the film and the music lover adds the music:

- The director sends you a video file.
- You watch the film and give the learners feedback on their film, their performance and their pronunciation.

It is also vital to give the learners feedback on all the work they have done in the preparation stage, as the *process* is as important as, or even more so than, the final *product*.

When the learners have completed editing, and the final product is ready for review, they should publish it in a sharable format such as avi, wma – or another similar format.

Step 6 – Viewing

The films the different groups have created can be presented to the whole class, to peers from other classes or to parents.

It is important to try to make each screening as similar to a cinema experience as possible:
- Project the films onto a screen.
- Turn off the lights and black out the windows.

The films can even be made public on YouTube, Vimeo or other video-sharing sites. However, before making a film available on a public site it is necessary to get written permission from all the learners who appear in it (or their parents).

Step 7 – Evaluating

As the impact on *learning* is greater in the *process* of film-making than in the *product*, remember that the evaluation of the process of creating the film is as important as, or even more important than, the quality of the finished product.

As the film project is part of a foreign language course, it is essential that the learners are encouraged to focus on language and linguistic forms.

An effective way of addressing errors is to select words, expressions or sentences which the learners used incorrectly:
- During their pre-production tasks and while they performed the film-making task, you can draw their attention to those forms which prove problematic.
- During the evaluation stage, you can now focus on their language errors – to prevent them from developing fluency at the expense of accuracy.

While evaluating *language* is fairly objective, evaluating the quality of *creativity* in a film-making project can be very subjective, so it is necessary to have some broad objective criteria for the appraisal of quality in relation to creativity:
- *Is language used creatively?*
- *Is there a balance between technical competence and creativity?*
- *Is the film aesthetically pleasing?*
- *Do the images and sound work well together?*

The learners should also be encouraged to look critically at their project by reflecting on the film-making process and the choices they made.

This can be done by making an evaluation sheet, with elements such as those in the two different types of questionnaire opposite.

☐ *I enjoyed the film-making project.*

☐ *I collaborated with the other members of the team.*

☐ *I listened to the opinions of the other members of the team.*

☐ *The other members of the team listened to my opinion.*

☐ *If I could do the project again, I'd do some things differently.*

☐ *If I could do the project again, I'd do a lot of things differently.*

☐ *If I could do the project again, I'd do nearly everything differently.*

---

1 *How did the film-making project challenge you linguistically?*

2 *How did your reading, writing and speaking skills improve during the film-making project?*

3 *How did the project challenge you intellectually?*

4 *How did you develop any research, planning or coordination skills during the film-making project?*

5 *How did you improve your critical thinking and decision-making skills during the project?*

6 *How did your self-confidence using new technology increase during the film-making project?*

7 *How did the project give you an opportunity to be creative?*

8 *What was the best thing about the project?*

9 *What was the worst thing about the project?*

10 *What additional comments and suggestions do you have about the film-making project?*

'I think that stories and the telling of stories
are the foundations of human communication
and understanding.

If children all over the country are watching films,
asking questions and telling their stories,
then the world will eventually be a better place.'

Beeban Kidron, film director

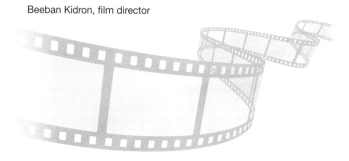

From the editors

Film in Action is a book by someone who is passionate about film – and who knows a lot about film. But Kieran also knows a lot about being an English teacher, and has a great deal of experience incorporating film successfully into his classrooms.

As the moving image becomes more dominant in our society, film and learner-created film are becoming a central focus in the classroom – and this is one of the ambitious goals of Kieran's book:

- His learners first take an exploratory look at film itself, respond to films, speak about them, write about them, imagine their own films and write their own scripts.
- His learners then move on to creating their own films.

Kieran's classes place the moving image at the centre of the language learning agenda.

Part A introduces us to different aspects of film: how it can inspire, while exposing our learners to a wide range of authentic language, aiding comprehension, improving intercultural understanding and fomenting visual literacy.

Part B is filled with activities, moving from actively watching film to actively producing film. The activities are clearly set out – you read them and immediately understand them – and mix highly original ideas with more reassuringly 'classical' procedures.

Part C takes us beyond the classroom and into the school system, by way of longer, more complex projects – where film takes on increased protagonism – that demonstrate how we are very much part of the age of visual information.

Film in Action is a highly fascinating invitation for us, as teachers, to take a fresh look at a fast-developing medium, and to invite our students along for the journey.

Mike Burghall
Lindsay Clandfield

DELTA TEACHER DEVELOPMENT SERIES

A pioneering award-winning series of books for English Language Teachers with professional development in mind.

Film in Action
by Kieran Donaghy
ISBN 978-1-909783-07-2

Teaching children how to learn
by Gail Ellis and Nayr Ibrahim
ISBN 978-1-905085-86-6

Going Mobile
by Nicky Hockly and Gavin Dudeney
ISBN 978-1-909783-06-5

Storytelling With Our Students
by David Heathfield
ISBN 978-1-905085-87-3

The Autonomy Approach
by Brian Morrison and Diego Navarro
ISBN 978-1-909783-05-8

Spotlight on Learning Styles
by Marjorie Rosenberg
ISBN 978-1-905085-71-2

The Book of Pronunciation
by Jonathan Marks and Tim Bowen
ISBN 978-1-905085-70-5

The Company Words Keep
by Paul Davis and Hanna Kryszewska
ISBN 978-1-905085-20-0

Digital Play
by Kyle Mawer and Graham Stanley
ISBN 978-1-905085-55-2

Teaching Online
by Nicky Hockly with Lindsay Clandfield
ISBN 978-1-905085-35-4

Teaching Unplugged
by Luke Meddings and Scott Thornbury
ISBN 978-1-905085-19-4

Culture in our Classrooms
by Gill Johnson and Mario Rinvolucri
ISBN 978-1-905085-21-7

The Developing Teacher
by Duncan Foord
ISBN 978-1-905085-22-4

Being Creative
by Chaz Pugliese
ISBN 978-1-905085-33-0

The Business English Teacher
by Debbie Barton, Jennifer Burkart and Caireen Sever
ISBN 978-1-905085-34-7

For details of these and future titles in the series, please contact the publisher: *E-mail* info@deltapublishing.co.uk
Or visit the DTDS website at www.deltapublishing.co.uk/titles/methodology